THE COMPLETE
CRICUT® MACHINE
HANDBOOK

THE COMPLETE CRICUT® MACHINE HANDBOOK

A Beginner's Guide to Creative Crafting with Vinyl,
Paper, Infusible Ink and More!

ANGIE HOLDEN

CREATOR OF THE COUNTRY CHIC COTTAGE

PAGE STREET
PUBLISHING CO.

PAGE STREET
PUBLISHING CO.

First published in 2022 by
Page Street Publishing Co.
27 Congress Street, Suite 1511
Salem, MA 01970
www.pagestreetpublishing.com

Distributed by Macmillan, sales in Canada by The Canadian Manda Group.

Cricut® is a registered trademark of Cricut, Inc., which was not involved in the creation of this book.

26   25   24   23   22   1   2   3   4   5

ISBN-13: 978-1-64567-651-5
ISBN-10: 1-64567-651X

Library of Congress Control Number: 2022936161

Cover and book design by Rosie Stewart for Page Street Publishing Co.
Photography by Angie Holden

Printed and bound in the United States

Page Street Publishing protects our planet by donating to nonprofits like The Trustees, which focuses on local land conservation.

CONTENTS

HELLO AND WELCOME!

You are entering the exciting world of Cricut®! You may feel overwhelmed, confused and even unclear on where to begin. I am here to help you! I have been creating my entire life; after I discovered craft cutting machines over a decade ago, I've been hooked ever since.

I am passionate about teaching and inspiring others to use their Cricut machines through my blog and YouTube channel. Now I'm taking that one step further and giving you a printed handbook that you can use to learn everything you need to know about your machine.

This book will walk you through a variety of projects, each of which teaches you a new skill with your Cricut machine. Start with the preliminary sections that highlight essential materials and basic Cricut techniques, then move on to the projects. To get the most from this guide, you should work through each project in order, as each one builds your skills as well as your confidence. By the end of this book, you will be ready to tackle any Cricut project you can imagine!

Need to skip to a specific skill quickly? Reference the index (page 186) for the location of tutorials in this book. Remember that not every machine has the capability to make every project. Pick the projects that use your machine and build your skill set as you create.

Remember that all screenshots of Cricut Design Space® in this book are of a PC computer and will be similar on a Mac. You can also find an app for mobile and tablet; however, not all functions will be available. There are notes about which operations cannot be used on mobile; however, no specific mobile instructions are included. Also, Cricut often makes changes to the interface so things may look slightly different on your end depending on when you purchased this book.

Ready to start creating? You will need the project files and material sources, and you can find those at cricuthandbook.com. You will need to upload these files to Cricut Design Space for some of the projects. All files are for personal use only, and you can read more about licensing on page 31.

Get ready to learn both your machine and Cricut Design Space. From the very first project, you will be making gorgeous creations just like you see on Pinterest and your favorite craft blogs. Get that Cricut machine out of the box and start making things for yourself, to give as gifts and even to sell. I know that you can make amazing things with your machine!

Happy creating!

Welcome to Cricut Setup

Select a product type to continue.

Smart Cutting Machine

Heat Press

GETTING STARTED

Do you have a brand-new Cricut machine? Open that box and let's get started. Inside you will find your machine and some cords, as well as some materials. There should also be a "get started" guide that gives you a website address. Head to that website to begin the setup process. That process will actually guide you through downloading Cricut Design Space as well as making your very first cuts. Cricut Design Space is the application that will communicate with your machine, and this book will help walk you through how to use it.

You will need to either use the provided cord to connect your machine to your computer or connect via Bluetooth®. The cord connects to a USB port on your computer and can be used with any Cricut except the Joy™. Bluetooth is a wireless way to connect your machine and is standard on the Joy, Explore Air® 2, Explore® 3, Maker® and Maker® 3. You may need to use passcode 0000 to connect for the first time.

If for some reason you get lost in this process and can't seem to find the website, head to design.cricut.com to download Cricut Design Space. Open the program and click the three lines in the upper left-hand corner. Click "new product setup" to get started. This will register your product and get it ready for use.

Once you are done with the machine setup, you are ready to start learning more about your machine. Just continue with this book to get creative and make some projects, all while learning the functions of Design Space and your Cricut machine.

CRICUT BASICS, MATERIALS AND TOOLS

Whether you are purchasing your first Cricut machine or have had a machine for years, you will need to know a few basics before getting started. Let's start with a brief machine explanation, then move on to the materials and tools that you may want to consider.

CRICUT MACHINES

There is currently a wide range of Cricut machines on the market that are all slightly different. Have no fear! This book has projects that work with every machine type. Want to expand your Cricut collection or upgrade? Here is a brief description of each machine. Remember there is no wrong answer here! All of the Cricut machines are amazing. You just need to find the one that is right for you.

CRICUT JOY

The Cricut Joy is small and easy to use, making it perfect for beginners. It is also great for those who have space constraints or want to travel with their machine. However, this machine can only cut lightweight materials and you will not be able to make Print Then Cut projects like those on pages 153 to 165 or add score lines to your material. Otherwise, you can draw or add foil lines to your project just like the other machines! Please note that all of the tools and pens are specific to the Joy.

When using your Joy, keep in mind the size limits as you may need to alter some projects. For material on a mat, the maximum cutting area is 4.25 x 11.75 inches (10.6795 x 29.44 cm). You do have the option of cutting Cricut Smart Materials without a mat up to 4.5 inches (11.253 cm) wide and 4 feet (1.22 m) long for a single cut or up to 20 feet (6.1 m) long for repeated cuts.

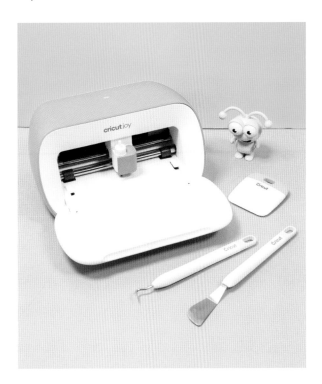

CRICUT EXPLORE

The Cricut Explore Air 2 and Explore 3 are the current models on the market as of 2022, but this series also includes the Explore and Explore One. These machines can cut a wider range of materials than the Cricut Joy, especially materials that are slightly thicker since you have the option of adding the deep point blade. Plus, you will love making Print Then Cut projects and even adding score lines to your cards. Add pens or even the foil tool to your collection for additional options when creating.

When cutting on a mat, you can go up to 11.5 x 23.5 inches (29.21 x 59.69 cm). The Explore 3 has the ability to cut Cricut Smart Materials without a mat, and those can go up to 11.75 inches (29.84 cm) wide and 12 feet (3.5 m) long. The maximum size for any Print Then Cut project is 6.75 x 9.25 inches (17.145 x 23.495 cm).

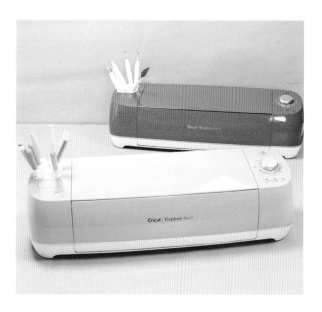

CRICUT MAKER

The Cricut Maker is the most powerful Cricut machine on the market. The Maker series of machines includes the Maker and the Maker 3. They did skip a number in this series, so there is no Maker 2 machine. These machines are the top of the line and do the most of any Cricut machine currently on the market. A Maker can do anything any of the other machines can do and so much more! This includes cutting fabric like a dream and diving into thick materials like basswood, chipboard and even leather.

The Maker series can use any of the Explore blades, plus a special series of blades just for these machines. That means you can cut thicker materials, engrave, deboss and so much more! The projects in this book will teach you how to use most of the tools and give you ideas for creating with them. Just keep any projects you create in the same size restrictions as mentioned for the Explore series and decide which projects you will tackle first!

CRICUT MACHINE PARTS

Let's take a tour of a typical Cricut machine and what each part is called. On the outside of the Explore and Maker machines, you will find various buttons. The Cricut Joy actually does not have any buttons. The button appearance and location are dependent on the machine you have, but here is a quick rundown:

- **Power button:** The power button is used to turn the machine on and off.

- **Unload/load button:** This button is indicated by an arrow and used to load or unload the mat from the machine.

- **Go button:** This looks like either the Cricut "C" symbol or a triangle play symbol. Press this to start your cut.

- **Pause button:** Pause is indicated by two lines and will temporarily stop the machine in the middle of a cut.

- **Dial:** Explore Air 2 and earlier machines also have a material setting dial. You can choose a material from here or leave it on custom to choose from a more comprehensive list in Cricut Design Space.

- **Open button:** Only the Explore series has an additional button for opening your machine. With other machines, you just pull to open instead of pushing a button.

- **Cartridge slot:** Explore Air 2 and earlier machines will also have a slot where you can add cartridges. These are obsolete technology for older machines that stored images. You can use this slot to connect the cartridges to your account. For newer machines, contact Cricut customer service if you have cartridges and they can assist you with accessing those.

- **USB port and power cord connection:** You can find these slots on the back of your Cricut machine; however, you can also use Bluetooth connection with current Cricut models.

The inside of a Cricut machine has the carriage, which is where the clamps are located. The clamps are what will hold the blades and pens inside the machine. The Cricut Joy only has one clamp, while the Explore and Maker series have two clamps (A and B). This carriage rides along a silver roller bar.

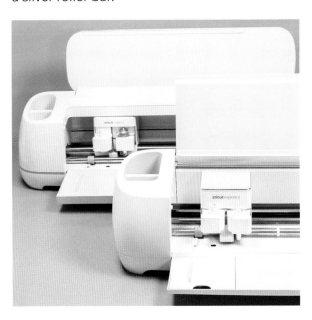

There is an additional roller bar that has some white star wheels all along the length. These will need to be moved for thicker materials or those that mar easily. Power off your machine and move the carriage out of the way. Then push the star wheels all the way over to the right. This is fairly easy to do on new models but the older Explore models can be a pain. The wheels will move with enough effort!

The roller also has some gray wheels on both sides for guiding your mats. These are not to be moved and need to stay in location. You will also notice white mat guides on the sides of the machine. You will place the mat under these and against these gray rollers when loading.

You will also find that your Cricut Explore or Maker machine has some built-in storage. From cups on the side to a tray that opens, you are able to store a few things right inside your machine. The Cricut Joy does not have any of these storage features.

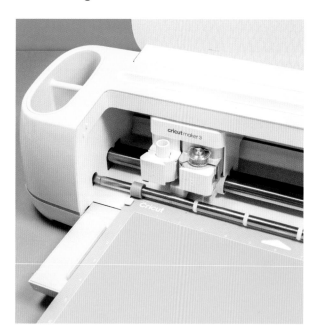

The Cricut Maker 3

CRICUT MATERIALS

There are so many materials out there that your Cricut machine can cut! In fact, the Cricut Maker has over 300 materials listed. Each machine is different, of course, but there is a wide variety that will cut on each one. I tried to choose commonly used materials for this book. Here is a quick glimpse at what you can cut with your Cricut:

- Paper
- Vinyl
- HTV (Heat Transfer Vinyl)
- Infusible Ink™
- Stencil materials
- Fabric
- Wood
- Printable materials
- And other specialty materials like leather, craft foam and metal

You do not have to purchase materials from the Cricut brand. Your Cricut machine will cut any materials in a particular family no matter what brand makes them. For example, you can cut Cricut or Siser® HTV. However, for each new brand of material, you may find that you need to play around and find the right cut settings. Generally, the cut settings are intended for the Cricut brand and may need some adjustment with other brands for a successful cut.

CRICUT BLADES

All Cricut machines come with the fine point blade; however, you may want to purchase additional blades as you expand your crafting knowledge. This can get a bit confusing, and you don't want to waste your money purchasing the wrong ones. Use this guide to determine which blades work with your machine and any housings you may have.

CRICUT JOY BLADES

The Cricut Joy machine comes with the fine point blade and you can purchase an optional foil tool separately. The housings and blades are different from any other Cricut machine so you want to make sure you get tools that are marked for the Cricut Joy.

CRICUT EXPLORE BLADES

All Explore machines come with a fine point blade. You also have the option of purchasing the deep point blade, bonded fabric blade and foil tool. The deep and fine point blades are two different angles so they are completely different. The bonded fabric blade is just the fine point blade in a pink housing. Similar to having different scissors for fabric, it is a good idea to keep a blade just for fabric, and the pink color helps you keep the blades separate. The foil tool comes in a kit with three interchangeable tips for fine, medium and bold lines.

Fine Point Blade (3), Bonded Fabric Blade (4), Deep Point Blade (5), Tips for Foil Tool (6), Foil Tool (7)

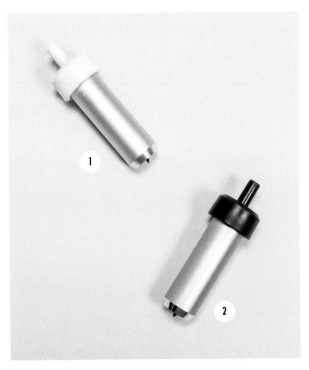

Cricut Joy Fine Point Blade (1), Cricut Joy Foil Tool (2)

CRICUT MAKER BLADES

The Maker machines have the most blade options, which can get a bit confusing. First, the Maker will take any blades available for the Explore machine (page 13). All Maker machines come with a fine point blade, and you can purchase the others if you need them. I actually do not recommend the bonded fabric blade for the Maker. Instead, I use the rotary blade discussed in the next paragraph for cutting all fabric.

There are also blades that work only with the Maker. The Maker has a special adaptive tool system that the other machines do not have. The rotary blade comes with the original Maker but is not included with the Maker 3. It is a round blade that cuts similarly to a rotary cutter for fabric but it is much smaller. This blade has its own housing. The knife blade also has its own housing and is like a craft knife for your Cricut Maker. It is purchased separately and will cut thick materials like basswood, leather, chipboard and more.

The other tips you can purchase for the Cricut Maker all work with the QuickSwap™ housing. That means you can use the one housing and use as many or as few of these tips as you would like. There are single and double scoring wheels, engraving, debossing, wavy and perforation tips that all fit on this housing. On these tips you will find numbers to help keep you from getting them confused. These are 01 single scoring wheel, 02 double scoring wheel, 11 perforation blade, 21 debossing tip, 31 wavy blade and 41 engraving tip.

Please note that for safety reasons, the plastic covering over the gear on top of the Maker blades should remain in place. The rotary and knife blade also have a plastic cover over the blade itself, and these covers can be removed when cutting and replaced when storing.

The Maker series also has a feature that checks if you have the correct blade loaded. The carriage that holds the blades will move to the right at the beginning of the cut as the machine runs a check. It will display on your screen if you have the wrong blade loaded. A typical mistake is to confuse the scoring wheels with the rotary blade. Be sure to take note if your machine indicates an error, and check that you have the correct blade loaded.

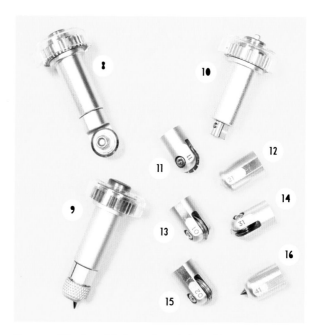

Rotary Blade with Housing (8), Knife Blade with Housing (9), QuickSwap Housing (10), Perf Tip (11), Deboss Tip (12), Single Scoring Wheel (13), Wavy Tip (14), Double Scoring Wheel (15), Engraving Tip (16)

CHANGING YOUR CRICUT BLADE

The blades on your Cricut machine do not have to be changed as often as you think. If your machine is not cutting correctly, try a new or clean mat first. You will also want to pull out your blade and clean it occasionally. An easy way to do this is to make a ball of aluminum foil and insert the blade several times to remove residue and debris.

If you find your blade is still not cutting correctly, you can change it out and add a new blade to the same housing. Replacement blades are easy to remove and add. For the fine point, deep point and foil tool, depress the plunger on top to remove the blade, then put a new one inside. The blade is magnetic so it will go right into the correct location.

The rotary and knife blade are a bit more complicated to change; however, instructions come with the replacement blades and walk you through the process. If your rotary blade is skipping places in the cut, it is time to change it, as those blades do nick easily. The knife blade will also get dull and sometimes even break when you are cutting.

The tips for the QuickSwap housing will probably never need replacement but it is super simple to swap between tips. Just press down the plunger on the top of the housing. Remove one tip and add another, then release the plunger.

CALIBRATING CRICUT BLADES

The rotary and knife blade both have calibration options in Cricut Design Space. Please note that your Cricut Maker will automatically run the first calibration when you install these blades.

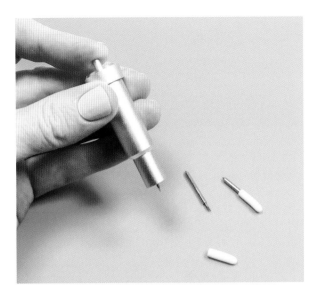

You can manually run another if you feel your cuts are off or if you want to double-check the alignment. To do that, click the three lines in the upper left-hand corner and choose "calibration." Then pick what type of calibration you want to perform and your computer will walk you through the rest. Currently, blade calibration is not available on the mobile app.

CRICUT MATS

In addition to blades, Cricut mats are another important tool for using your Cricut machine. All Cricut machines can cut materials on a mat. The Joy, Explore 3 and Maker 3 can cut Cricut Smart Materials with no mat required. Otherwise, you will need some type of mat to cut any material. Here are the grip strengths of the Cricut mats:

- **Fabric grip:** pink mat that has the lightest grip, mainly for fabric crafts

- **Light grip:** light blue mat that is used for a ton of thin materials

- **Standard grip:** green mat that has a slightly stronger grip than blue

- **Strong grip:** purple mat that has the strongest grip of any mat

- **Card mat:** special blue mat that cuts pre-cut and folded cards

These options can get confusing! Use the guide on page 18 as a quick reference to picking the right mat for the right material. Also, each material chapter will guide you in your mat choice.

Note: *When referencing mat sizes above, the size is the sticky area of the mat, not the overall size.*

The Cricut Joy can only use the Joy mats that are either 4.5 x 6.5 inches (11.4 x 16.5 cm) or 4.5 x 12 inches (11.4 x 30.5 cm). These only come in light, standard and the special card mat version. All other Cricut machines have the option of a 12 x 12–inch (30.5 x 30.5–cm) mat or a 12 x 24–inch (30.5 x 61–cm) mat in all four grip strengths. You can also get a card mat that cuts up to 4 pre-cut folded cards at one time. All mats have dimensions printed on them in inches as well as centimeters.

The condition of your mat has a direct effect on the quality of your cut. When your mat gets dirty and worn it will not hold your material in order for the Cricut to cut correctly. If you are having issues getting your material to stick to the mat, I recommend cleaning the sticky area with plain water and a little bit of dish soap. Then use a scraper to remove dirt and debris. Allow your mat to dry and you should get several more cuts from it.

The pink fabric mat does have a different adhesive type than the other mats. I recommend just using some strong grip transfer tape on it to pick up dirt and debris. The washing method for other mats will not work for these, as you don't want to scrape off the adhesive. Use caution when using the pink mat and do not touch the adhesive with your fingers. The oils from your hands can break it down and shorten the mat's life.

Want to make your mats last even longer? All Cricut mats except for card mats are reversible, so you can use both sides. Alternate the direction you put the mat into the machine so you are not cutting over the same area multiple times. You can also make your mats last longer by using them as lighter grip mats as they wear. For example, a really worn green mat can be used as a blue mat in a pinch.

A new mat can be really tough on certain materials. New mats are super sticky, and I have seen them rip some papers. If you are having issues, stick the new mat to your shirt a few times before using it. That should pick up a small amount of lint and prevent your material from sticking too aggressively to the mat's surface.

All Cricut mats come with a clear protective cover over the sticky surface. Always remove this before adding your material. You will also want to add this cover back after each use. Always store your mats with the clear protective cover in place to prevent dirt and debris from getting on the surface.

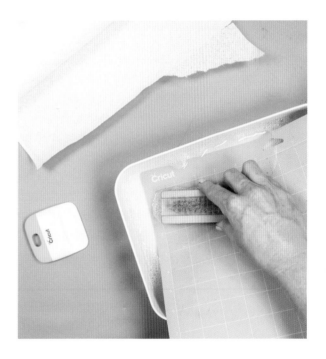

CRICUT MAT GUIDE

PINK FABRIC MAT

- Any fabric
- Tissue paper
- Crepe paper

NOTE: Adhesive is different from other mats. Avoid touching it with your hands. Clean by applying strong grip transfer tape over the surface to pull up debris.

LIGHT GRIP MAT

- Printer paper
- Vinyl
- Iron-on
- Thin cardstock
- Vellum
- Construction paper
- Washi sheets
- Wood veneer
- Wrapping paper

STANDARD GRIP MAT

- Cardstock
- Pattern paper
- Embossed cardstock
- Iron-on
- Vinyl
- Infusible Ink transfer sheets
- Faux leather and suede
- Felt
- Poster board

STRONG GRIP MAT

- Thick cardstock
- Glitter cardstock
- Magnet material
- Chipboard
- Leather
- Mat board
- Balsa and Basswood
- Corrugated cardboard
- Cork
- Craft foam

CARD MAT

- Cut and pre-folded cards

CLEANING

Use plain water and a bit of dish soap. Scrub the mat with a brush. Use a scraper to get off excess dirt.

CRICUT PENS AND MARKERS

Want to draw with your Cricut instead of cut? You can add Cricut pens or markers to any Cricut machine to draw lines instead of cutting them. These can be used for single line writing or creating outlines. Currently, there is not a fill option built into Design Space so you cannot color in your design with your machine.

The pens for the Cricut Joy are different from those that are for the Explore and Maker series. Be sure to look on the package for markings that indicate which machine they are for. Cricut Design Space will prompt you when the pens are needed. For the Joy, the machine will pause for the pen to be added to the same clamp as the blade. For the other machines, the A clamp is for pens while the B clamp is for blades.

There is also a wide variety of pens and markers to choose from. This includes various widths as well as types, like gel, metallic, glitter, Infusible Ink and more. There is even a washable fabric pen for marking fabric with sewing pattern marks and more. Pick and choose the color and type that works best with the project that you have in mind.

ADDITIONAL CRICUT TOOLS

You can purchase many tools to go with your Cricut machine. I am going to cover the ones that are important for beginners. You can add more as you find you need them for various projects.

A brayer is a tool that I personally cannot live without, and I recommend it to all new Cricut users. This tool will help you to push your material into the mat adhesive, getting a better grip and extending the life of your mats.

Weeding tools will be needed if you are going to use vinyl or HTV. With these materials, you need to remove all of the excess material, and weeding tools help you to do that easily. I find that each individual has a preference as to which weeding tool is best. A variety pack will help you narrow down your favorite, or you can just go with a single hook to start out. In my opinion, all brands work the same so pick one that you like to get started.

In addition to more traditional hook weeding tools, many people like to use tweezers when weeding. Tweezers can also be handy when lifting small items off of the mat or gripping small cuts of paper.

A scraper is required for vinyl projects as you will need it for burnishing. There are a variety of sizes that you can choose from depending on your preference or the size of your project. You can also find felt-covered ones that are great for specialty vinyl that may become scratched.

The scoring stylus is a must if you want to add fold lines to your projects in the Explore series of machines. For the Maker, you can go with the scoring wheels mentioned in the blade section (page 14), or the stylus will work with this machine as well.

A spatula is nice to have but definitely not required. You can use it to get under paper pieces to lift them off of the mat. This is especially handy for picking up and removing scrap pieces. A scraper can be used in place of this most of the time, so this tool is optional.

If you have trouble seeing the cut lines on vinyl or HTV, I recommend buying a light box. This has the same function as holding your material up to a bright window but the box itself makes it super convenient. By illuminating the material from the back, the cut lines will be easier to see and it will make your crafting so much more enjoyable!

Cricut makes a roll holder attachment that only works with the Explore 3 and Maker 3. It is designed to hold large rolls of Smart Vinyl™ and Smart Iron-On™ when cutting without a mat. It really is a great addition if you have either of these two machines.

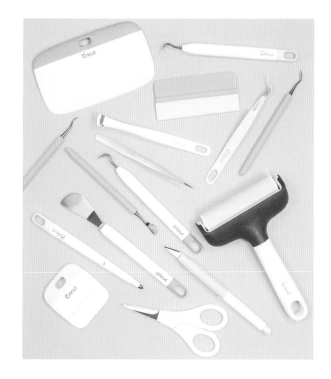

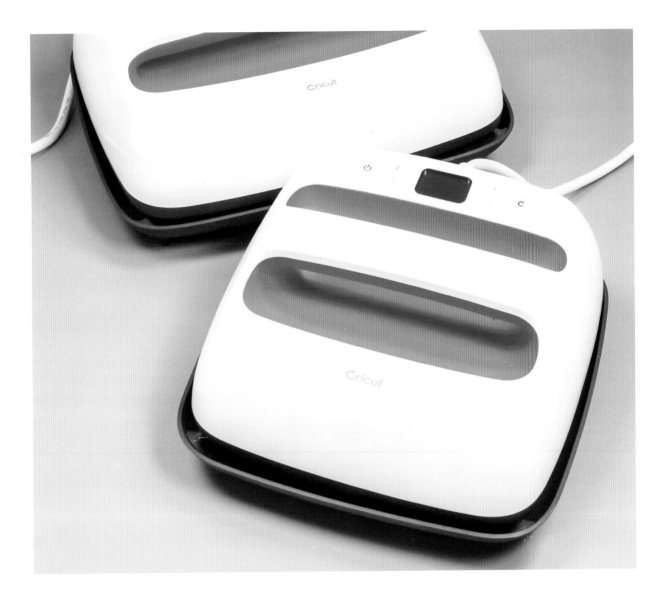

HEAT SOURCES AND ACCESSORIES

When adding HTV to a shirt or even Infusible Ink to coasters, you will need a heat source for application. You can choose from a wide variety of options depending on your needs and budget. Here are a few of the most popular:

- **Household iron:** You may already have an iron that will work for applying HTV or doing sewing projects. However, the heat from an iron is not very consistent, so if you find you are having issues getting HTV to stick, it may very well be because of your heat source. Also, an iron will not work for Infusible Ink, as it does not get hot enough.

- **Cricut EasyPress™:** This small handheld press works wonders for HTV application and also gets hot enough for Infusible Ink projects. I have only used the Cricut version but there are other brands on the market.

- **Cricut Mug Press™:** This specialty machine is used for applying Infusible Ink to mugs and some tumblers. Other brands of mug and tumbler presses will perform the same function.

- **Heat presses:** If you want to go more professional, you may want to add a heat press to your crafting area. These larger presses allow for better control of pressure and are often easier to use for some specialty materials. Plus you no longer have to hold down your EasyPress when making a project! You can also find heat presses for other applications, including hats, balls and so much more.

- **Convection oven:** There is an option to purchase a small countertop oven for your craft room and use it for your projects like mugs, tumblers and more. These are great for small items and for those who want an affordable alternative to multiple heat presses and attachments for specific blanks.

You do not have to invest in these tools from the beginning. Start small and work your way up as you see a need or have a desire to expand your crafting. You may find that crafting with an iron works well for you and the crafts that you enjoy making!

There are a few accessories that you may want to consider along with your heat source. The most important of those is a pressing mat. These are used to press on and protect your work surface. You can use a folded towel here or invest in something like an EasyPress mat or one of the other brands on the market. I like to keep several sizes of these on hand for adding to the inside of my projects.

The other accessory that I highly recommend is a Teflon™ sheet. This can be used for HTV projects to protect the material of your blank or the other layers of HTV from your heat source. Although not required, these are handy, especially for more complicated HTV designs and project ideas. I especially like to use them if I am working with delicate material or if I am not sure of the material that I am working with. You can use parchment paper in place of this in a pinch.

CRICUT DESIGN SPACE®

To use your Cricut, you will need Cricut Design Space either on a computer, tablet or mobile device. The computer version of Design Space has the most features and is generally what I recommend. You will download the program when setting up your machine and then make the first few cuts. This section of the book will give you a basic overview. I will go into detail on how to use the features of the program within each of the projects, so be sure to work your way through each section in order.

Note: There are minimum operating system requirements for Cricut Design Space, which can be found on the Cricut website. You will need an internet connection to get started, but you can save things for offline use.

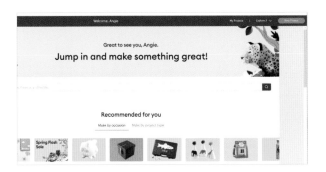

CRICUT ACCESS™

Design Space is a free program and you do not have to pay a monthly fee. There is an optional subscription called Cricut Access™. Cricut Access gives you fonts, images and ready-to-make projects right in Cricut Design Space, plus a discount when purchasing materials. If you see a green "A" in Design Space, that indicates a Cricut Access item. Every crafter is different, and some love Cricut Access while others do not. I generally find that over time you will discover which option works best for you. You may also want to read Cricut Angel Policy and Copyright Information (page 31), as that is another reason to get a subscription.

GETTING TO KNOW DESIGN SPACE

For now, the terms in Design Space may be a bit confusing! Each chapter and project of this book will work through the elements and explain each of the functions. Don't stress about learning it all at once! It takes time to master Design Space and create like a pro, but you will get there. For now, open up the program and let's take a look around.

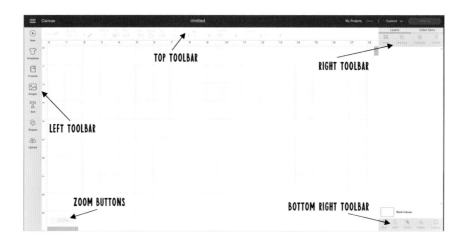

Click the "new project" button to get started. You will see what is referred to as your "canvas"; this is where you create a design. You can start playing with some of the features if you would like to orient yourself. Let's walk through just a few of the basic elements so that you are familiar with the workspace.

At any time, you can click the three lines in the upper left-hand corner to get a dropdown menu. From here, you can go back home or back to your canvas. This is also where Print Then Cut calibration (page 156) is located. A few other functions here will be discussed later in the book.

TOOLBARS

For the purpose of this book, I will be referring to each of the toolbars in Design Space as indicated in the image above. Remember that these toolbars only appear in these locations on the desktop or computer version of Design Space and may be elsewhere on other versions.

On the left toolbar, you will find things like ready-to-make projects, phrases and images. These are preloaded into Cricut Design Space and can be used at any time. You can click these and explore a bit now. Some of the images will be used for the crafts in this book. This toolbar also has the "new" button where you can start a new project at any time.

At the bottom of your screen, you will see an option to "zoom." This is nice when creating so you can zoom in to see smaller details. The bottom and right side also have bars that can be used to scroll around the canvas for larger projects.

The top toolbar has two very important features. On the left, you will always find "undo" and "redo." These are especially handy when you make a mistake. Click "undo" to reverse the last action you took in Design Space. The "redo" button will renew that action if you would like to put it back. I find I use these buttons all of the time, as mistakes do happen!

The right toolbar has your layers and color sync panel, as well as several functions on the bottom right toolbar. Again, each of these will be covered in detail in later sections. Two buttons that you will use a lot are the "duplicate" and "delete" buttons. These can be used to make copies of any object or to remove the object from your canvas completely.

Also, along the top, you will find a machine selection dropdown. Always be sure to choose the right machine type in Design Space. This selection will determine which functions appear on your screen. You may not be able to connect with your machine if the right type is not selected. Double-check this setting when you are working in Design Space.

HANDLES

When you highlight any item on your canvas, you will see four circles or handles. The "X" will remove or delete the object when clicked. The circular arrow allows you to rotate the object by clicking and holding it down then moving around. Resize any object with the double arrow by clicking, holding down and moving around the canvas. When the lock is closed, the height and width will both change at the same time. If you open the lock and resize, you can

distort the item by changing the height and width independently of each other. When you unlock the object, the double arrow button will change to a four-way arrow.

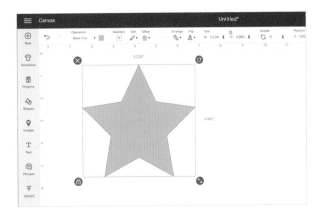

SAVING PROJECTS

Along the top, you will find the "save" button. You can use this at any time to save your project. Once you click this, you can add any name you would like and also divide your projects into collections if you would like. These collections help to organize your crafts so you can find them later. The number of collections is limited if you don't have Cricut Access.

Once you have some projects saved, you can click "my projects" at the top to find all of the projects you have saved. They are organized with the most recent first. You can use the collections on the left-hand side to sort them if needed. You can also click the "share" button to send your project to others. Please note that sharing only works if the project is made of fonts and images in Cricut Design Space. If you use your own fonts or upload images, sharing will not work.

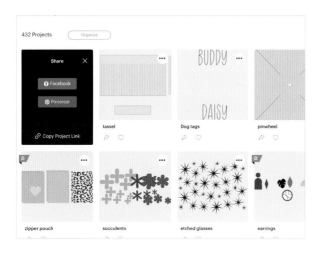

From here, you can click on a project to open it. Click "customize" to open on your canvas or click "make it" to go directly to cutting.

BASIC CUTTING INSTRUCTIONS

When you are ready to cut, the same basic instructions apply to every project. You will click "make it" in the upper right-hand corner of your screen. For this example, I am using a few stars drawn with the shape function. Feel free to add those to your canvas if you want to walk through the steps.

You will get a screen that asks you if you will use a mat or not. Pick the appropriate choice for your project from this screen.

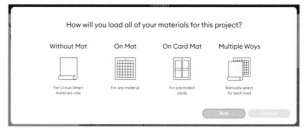

The next screen will show you the cuts that you are about to make. You can click "cancel" if something looks wrong or "continue" if you wish to cut. There are a few other options on this screen that will be covered in later chapters. For any paid files or fonts, you do not have to pay until you get to this screen and click "continue." That means you can add anything you like to your canvas to get an idea of how it will look. If there is an unexpected fee, click "checkout" to see the items, then go back to remove them if desired.

For even more options, click "browse all materials." You will only be able to pick "compatible" materials or those that Cricut says you can use with your machine and design. Use the search bar on this screen to narrow down the list. You can also click the star on any material to make it part of your personal favorites. Anything on this screen that has a Cricut "C" beside it was developed with the Cricut brand of materials. You can use those same settings for other brands; however, you may need to make some adjustments.

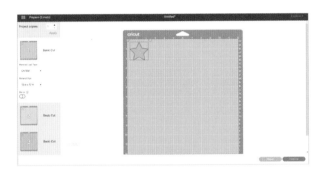

Once you click "continue," you will need to connect your machine, then it will ask you to pick a material. If you are using an Explore Air 2 or earlier, you can use the dial on the machine to pick a material or switch it to custom for a wider selection.

Once you have picked a material, you can fine-tune the pressure setting by choosing "more" or "less" pressure. It will be automatically set to "default." Use "more" or "less" on the dropdown to cut into the material slightly more or less, respectively. As a general rule, I use the default setting for cutting and only change it if I am having issues with the material.

On this screen, you will also see the option to "remember material settings." Checking this box will remember the material for each mat in your project. Design Space will tell you which tools it recommends for your specific project and design. You may also see some warnings on this screen. Things like moving the star wheels or mirroring your design are common. Always check these things when you are cutting to ensure you have either done what is suggested or you know that in your particular case that step is not needed.

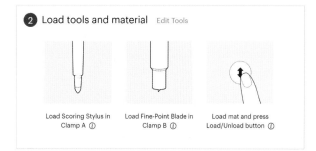

If there are other blade or tool options that you can use for a project, the "edit tools" will be clickable. Click this to see other options and pick one of those if they apply to you. You will not see this with all materials or designs.

Add the appropriate tools to the clamp(s). On the Joy, you will add any tool to the single clamp. Just drop in the tool and close the clamp. On the Explore and Maker, blades go in clamp B and pens, markers and the scoring stylus go in clamp A. Remember to hold clamp A from the bottom and push until the pen or stylus clicks.

Once you are ready to cut, you should see that the "unload/load" button is flashing on your machine. Hold your mat that has your material attached under the mat guides on both sides and against the gray rollers. Press the "unload/load" button while pushing on the mat at the same time. If you are using the Joy, the mat will load as soon as you put it in the machine without pushing any buttons.

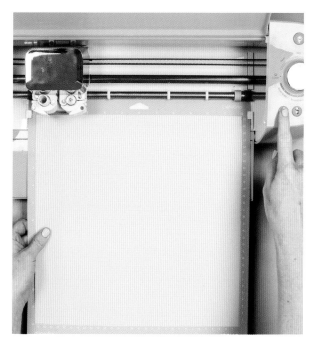

The machine will load the mat. It may check to make sure you have enough material depending on which machine you are using. Design Space will indicate it is ready to cut and tell you to press the "go" button. On the Explore Air 2 and original Maker, some materials will have a "fast mode" option to cut up to 2 times faster. You can experiment with turning this on if you would like. If you are having issues with your cuts, turn this feature off. Press the flashing "go" button on your machine to start your cut. For the Joy, you will press "go" in the application. Once pressed, the machine will start the cut. It may do some checks before starting the cut.

During the cut, you can press the "pause" button at any time to stop the machine. When you press "pause," Design Space will indicate your options on the screen. You can remove the mat by pressing the "unload/load" button, continue the cut from where it stopped by pressing "go" and even check the box on the screen to start the cut over from the beginning.

Paused

Choose an option below to continue.

Cancel
Press the Load/Unload button to unload material.

Resume
Press the Go button to resume.
☐ Resume from beginning

Once your cut is complete, Design Space will prompt you to unload the mat and the "unload/load" button will flash once more. Press this button to remove the mat. Once again, all of these functions will be in Design Space when using the Joy.

Once you press the button, the mat will eject from under the rollers and you can remove it. You can then remove the material from the mat. The best way to do this for most materials is to flip the mat over and peel the mat back from the material. This ensures that you do not damage or curl your material when peeling it off of the mat.

Design Space will then be ready for your next mat. The mat that is ready to be cut will be high-lighted. You can go back and cut a mat again simply by clicking on it. The "cancel" button in the lower right-hand corner will allow you to exit the cut at any time. This button will change to "finish" once you have completed all mats for the cut. Even if the button says "finish," you can go back and recut any mats that you need to on this screen by clicking on them.

You can also click "edit" on any mat on this screen if you forgot to do something previously. This may save you from needing to cancel your cut.

Once you are done crafting for the day, you can just turn your machine off to store it. I generally keep mine unplugged when not in use.

CRICUT DESIGN SPACE ISSUES

If you are having any issues with Design Space, try these steps first:

- Restart the program as well as your computer/device and Cricut machine. This will generally solve most issues.

- If you are using the mobile application, make sure what you are trying to do is compatible. Many options are only for computers.

- Design Space will give you various errors in the layers panel on the right-hand side if you are trying to do something that will not work. These will be indicated by an orange triangle. Click the triangle to see the error. If you try to click "make it" anyway, you will once again see an error message.

- Make sure you have selected the correct machine in Design Space to match your equipment.

- Cricut Design Space updates itself auto-matically but you can download a new version at design.cricut.com if you think you do not have the latest version.

- There are times when completely uninstall-ing and reinstalling the app will help any issues you are having.

- In Design Space, click the three lines in the upper left-hand corner and click "update firmware" while your machine is connected. This can fix issues you are having with your machine.

- Temporary glitches and bugs do happen within the software. You can find a "feedback" button by clicking the three lines in the upper left-hand corner to report those.

- A call to Cricut customer service may be required, especially if you think your situation is unique or something is majorly wrong.

CRICUT COPYRIGHT INFORMATION AND ANGEL POLICY

Copyright infringement is a serious crime. Every image that you find on the internet is someone's intellectual property. Always be sure to check for copyright and use information when using any files. Most files made for a Cricut will have either a personal or commercial license. A personal license means that you can only use the file to create things for yourself or to give as gifts. A commercial license expands to items that you may sell. Please be sure to read all licenses to ensure you comply with the rules of use.

For images and projects found in Cricut Design Space, you will need to consult the Cricut Angel Policy. This policy indicates what can be used commercially and where there are restrictions. You will want to take note of restrictions for licensed characters such as Disney, Marvel and so forth, as these have use limitations. This is one reason you may benefit from a Cricut Access subscription, as you get thousands of images that can be used commercially for one monthly fee.

FILE TYPES FOR UPLOADING

You will practice uploading files later (page 55), but I wanted to cover the file types for your reference. There are several different file types that you may see when working with your Cricut:

- SVG: This is the most common file for uploading to your Cricut. It is a graphics file that is best for cutting. On your computer, this file may appear as an HTML file; however, they will upload correctly.

- PNG: These types of files are great for doing Print Then Cut projects and often already have the background removed.

- JPG, GIF, BMP: These are all alternate photo files that will not have any background removed.

- DXF: This is another format for a cut file, but it is not as good as an SVG file for a Cricut machine. When given a choice, always use the SVG format.

- ZIP: This is an easy way to deliver multiple file types at once. You will need to unzip the file in order to get something you can upload to your Cricut. Open the zip file and you should see options to extract the individual files. Note that you do not need any paid service for zip files.

PAPER

Paper is a great place to get started when crafting with your Cricut machine. Paper is a versatile craft medium that comes in a wide variety of types and finishes. It is easy to find a paper that will work for your project and match the style that you are looking to achieve. Start with the basics here, then move on to making DIY Paper Gift Tags (page 37), Easy All-Occasion Cards (page 41), Paper Banner wth Foil Lines (page 47) and more, later in this chapter. Once you complete these paper crafts, you will be ready to move on to more materials and be more confident with your Cricut skills!

PAPER CRAFTING BASICS

PAPER TYPES AND FINISHES

Cardstock is generally referred to by a weight measurement (100 lb/270 gsm for example). The higher that weight measurement, the thicker the paper. Take this into consideration when choosing a paper for your project. For example, a thin paper that you would use in your printer may not be the best if you are making a box with it. On the other hand, a thick paper may be harder to bend into a shape. Try to choose the right paper for the project.

I always recommend purchasing high-quality paper. The number one issue I see when cutting paper with a Cricut is that people tend to pick low-quality paper that tears easily in their Cricut machines. I like cardstock from Bazzill, DCWV®, American Crafts™ and Cricut, to name a few. I tend to stay away from construction paper, dollar store paper or any other brand that gives me issues when cutting in my machine.

You can also find paper in a variety of prints, finishes and more. Look for a pattern that you love or even a metallic sheen. Using the pens to draw? Look for cardstock with a smooth finish for a cleaner look. You should also be aware that there are solid-core and white-core papers. A paper with a white core will appear white in the center if you look at the paper from the side. A paper with a solid core will appear to be one color throughout. Both types are useful, but if you have a certain look in mind for your project, be sure you pick the right paper type so your project looks good from all angles.

ADDING PAPER TO THE MAT

Paper will generally go on the blue light grip Cricut mat. One exception would be something delicate like tissue or crepe paper where you would want to use the pink fabric grip mat. On the other end of the spectrum, sometimes you need a stronger grip with thicker papers. Consider the green mat for glitter cardstock and any other paper that does not stick well to the blue mat. Add the paper face up to the mat using the gridlines as a guide and press it down well.

CUT SETTINGS FOR PAPER

You always want to pick the type of cardstock you are using from the list in Cricut Design Space. There are generic settings for light (65 lb/176 gsm), medium (80 lb/216 gsm) and heavy (100 lb/270 gsm or more) cardstock, as well as some more specific settings for things like foil and glitter paper. Pick the closest setting to your paper to start. You can always do a small test cut or change when you cut your second sheet if you find that setting does not work well. Remember, to get to the custom settings when using a Cricut Explore Air 2 or earlier, turn your dial to custom. As a general rule, you will always cut paper with a fine point blade. This is the blade that comes with every Cricut machine, so paper crafts are a great place to start creating.

PAPER GLUE RECOMMENDATIONS

Once you have your pieces cut, you will need some type of glue to assemble them. The last thing you want is wrinkles and ripples in your paper! Here are a few options I recommend:

- A dry adhesive is my number one recommendation. This includes tape runners, glue dots, foam tape and more. I find that most brands in this category are pretty good, but I love the ultra-thin version of the Glue Dots® brand.

- A great alternative for small pieces is the Xyron® sticker maker. These small machines apply adhesive in a thin layer to the entire back of your piece, ensuring that the paper sticks well and doesn't ripple once applied. This is similar to applying double-sided tape to the entire surface of your material.

- Stick glue can be a great alternative to liquid for paper crafters. It will reduce the risk of wrinkling and you can find versions that are just as permanent as the other options listed here. Try stick glue like Aleene's® Tacky Glue® or Elmer's® CraftBond®.

- If you really love liquid glue, a few alternatives work well with paper. My two favorite brands are Bearly Art and Art Glitter glue. The second may sound like something for glitter, but trust me—it works like a dream! I like to get both of these with the precision tip to make application easier; you can control the flow so you don't apply too much.

- Decoupage should be used if you need a protective coating over the top of your project. They even have outdoor and dishwasher-safe versions of Mod Podge® now.

Tip: *Look for archival-quality glue if you are working on scrapbooks or anything where you don't want the glue to yellow over time.*

PAPER TROUBLESHOOTING

Struggling with your paper crafts? Use the list below to troubleshoot your issue.

- Does your mat rip your paper? Although the light grip mat works great for paper, a new one can be a little strong for some varieties. Try sticking it to your shirt to make it a little less sticky.

- Intricate and small designs can be tough when cutting from paper. Be sure to try the "cardstock for intricate cuts" setting to get better results.

- Review the section on paper types (page 33). A low-quality paper or something like construction paper will probably not cut cleanly no matter which setting you choose.

- Once your cut is complete, flip your mat upside down and curl the mat back to keep the paper as flat as possible. This will eliminate curling in your final project.

- Be sure to check the stickiness of your mat and the condition of your blade if your paper is not cutting correctly. Clean your mat and/or blade and try cutting again.

- If the paper does not cut all the way through, try choosing a thicker setting like glitter cardstock. You can also use the "more" and "less" pressure settings (page 27).

BEYOND THE BASICS

Want to take paper crafting to the next level? There are so many things you can do with paper right in your Cricut machine to really make your projects stand out!

- Add score lines for folding (page 57).

- Write with pens (page 44).

- Add metallic foil lines and designs (page 47).

- Deboss a design or writing into the surface (Maker models only, page 55).

- Make perforated cuts (Maker models only).

- Cut lines in a wavy pattern (Maker models only).

Paper is such a versatile craft medium. You can go from really simple projects to more intricate ones as you gain confidence in your crafting skills. Grab some paper and turn on your machine, as it is time to start creating with your Cricut!

DIY PAPER GIFT TAGS

Level: Beginner

Machine requirements: Any Cricut machine

Skills: Designing with shapes, slice, duplicate and weld

Challenge: Add writing to your design after you complete the paper cards in the next lesson.

Supplies Needed

Cardstock (approximately 80 lb/216 gsm; see Paper Types and Finishes, page 33)

Light grip (blue) Cricut mat

Fine point blade

Tape runner or other adhesive (see Paper Glue Recommendations, page 34)

Ribbon

The best part about making these gift tags is that they use the shapes in Cricut Design Space. The shapes are always free to use, so they are a great place to start when learning your machine. Start out small with these gift tags and put a smile on anyone's face!

1. Open up Design Space and pick the "shapes" menu in the left toolbar. To make the tag shape, add a square. Click the square that you just added and click the lock to unlock the dimensions. You can now click and hold on the arrow to resize or type in a specific size in the toolbar at the top. I made mine 2.5 x 4 inches (6.4 x 10.2 cm).

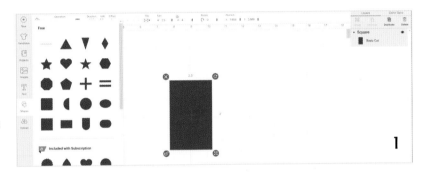

(continued)

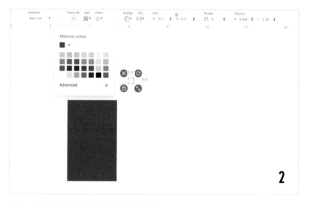

2

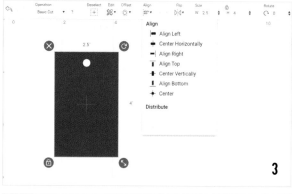

3

4

2. Add a circle shape and resize it to 0.3 inch (7.6 mm) or any other size that you feel will work. Remember that you will need a larger hole if the ribbon you want to use to attach your tag to your gift is of a larger size. A smaller hole will work for a smaller ribbon size.

Note: *You don't have to unlock this shape, as you want the size to remain consistent both vertically and horizontally.*

3. Click the small colored box next to "operation" on the top toolbar to change the circle to white so you can see the next steps. Click the circle and drag it to the approximate location on your tag. Then highlight *both* the rectangle and the circle and click "align" on the top toolbar. Then click "center horizontally" to make sure it is in the center.

4. While you have both objects still selected, click "slice" on the bottom right toolbar. You will be left with three layers. One is a tag with a hole and the other two are the original circle and the hole you sliced out. Click "delete" or the "X" on both circles to remove them.

Pro Tip: *You can only use slice when you have exactly two objects.*

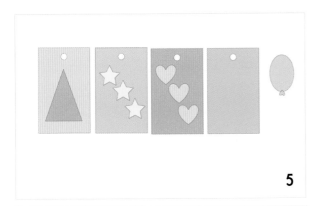

5

6

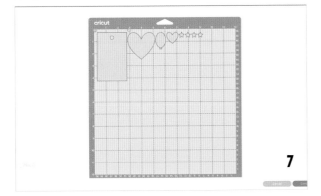

7

5. Then add more shapes to your canvas to design tags. Here I have added various stars, hearts and triangles. You can use the "duplicate" button to copy any shape. To make a balloon, add a circle and unlock. Then drag it until it is an oval. Add a small heart and use the arrow that looks like a circle to rotate it around. Put the heart on the bottom of the oval. Pick both the oval and the small heart and click "weld" in the bottom right toolbar. You now have a balloon!

6. Continue adding shapes and resizing them until you have a tag or tags that you like. Use the "arrange" button on the top toolbar to move objects to the front or back as needed. To make the bottom of the hat, I put several circles together and used the "weld" button as I did for the balloon previously. You can weld as many objects at one time as you would like.

Pro Tip: Change the color of any object so you can get a better idea of how your tags will look once complete. Be sure to make all of the objects that will be cut from one piece of paper the same color.

7. Once you are ready to cut, click "make it" to see the objects on your mats. You can see basic cutting instructions on page 26. Design Space will arrange your items to get the most from your paper. If you want the items to stay in place, see page 42 for information on the attach function.

8. Add the paper to the light grip mat and cut each piece with your Cricut machine. I used a medium cardstock setting to cut my pieces from each color of paper. See Adding Paper to the Mat (page 33) and Cut Settings for Paper (page 34).

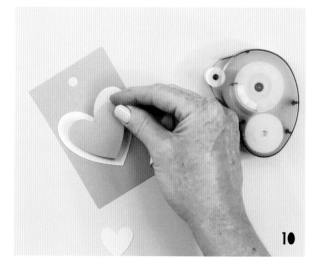

9. Once your pieces are cut, remove them from the mat. Be sure to peel the mat back from the material as shown on page 30. Repeat the cutting steps for each color of material.

10. Assemble your gift tags by placing adhesive on the back of each of the small pieces and putting them on the rectangle in the correct location.

11. Add a ribbon through the hole in the top and tie to complete your gift tag. You have just made a simple project with your Cricut machine! Just tie the gift tag onto your wrapped present or gift bag.

EASY ALL-OCCASION CARDS

Level: Beginner

Machine requirements: Any Cricut machine

Skills: Scoring lines, attach function, writing with pens, adding text

Challenge: After you make the Paper Banner with Foil Lines (page 47), come back and make some cards with foil lines.

Supplies Needed

Cardstock (approximately 80 lb/216 gsm) (see Paper Types and Finishes, page 33)

Light grip (blue) Cricut mat or card mat

Fine point blade

Scoring stylus or single scoring wheel (wheel is for the Maker only)

Tape runner or other adhesive (see Paper Glue Recommendations, page 34)

Insert card kit only if using card mat

Let's expand the use of shapes to make some cards. You can make cards for any occasion with your Cricut machine. Use pens to add writing on the outside or the inside of your cards as well. Have a card mat and want to make cards? Keep reading for instructions for other machines as well!

I. Open up Design Space and add a rectangle in the card size you want to make. Remember that you will fold these in half, so make sure the length is double what you want your final measurement to be. Typical cards start as 6 x 8 inches (15.2 x 20.53 cm) or 5 x 6 inches (12.7 x 15.2 cm) to make 4 x 6–inch (10.2 x 15.2–cm) and 3 x 5–inch (7.6 x 12.5–cm) cards. Pick the "shapes" menu on the left toolbar and pick a score line to add the line to your canvas. Resize the score line to be the full width of your card and rotate if needed.

(continued)

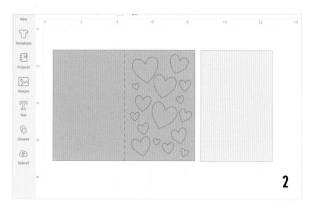

2

2. Now let's look at a few options to personalize your cards. You can add various shapes to the front of the card. Then pick the card, the score line and the shapes and click "attach" in the bottom right toolbar. The attach function will keep those items together on the mat, making your shapes cut out of the front of the card. You will also want to make another rectangle the same size as the front of your card. This is a simple way to start making cards on your Cricut.

3. Want to add text instead? Click the "text" button on the left toolbar and type your words.

3

4. Then pull down the "font" box on the top tool-bar to get to your font options. "System fonts" are those on your device, while "Cricut fonts" are those you can get from Cricut. Pick a font you like and your words will change to that font. If any of your fonts are missing, uncheck the "kerned fonts only" box and they will probably appear.

5. Resize as needed and add the text to the front of your card. Pick everything and click "attach" to cut this out from the front. Again, I made a rectangle the same size as the front to add to the card after cutting.

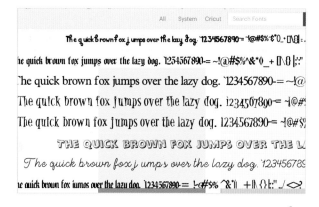

4

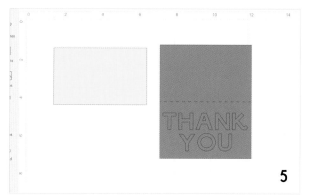

5

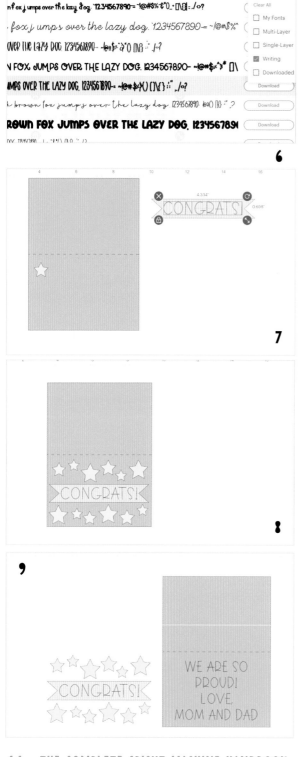

6. Let's do a third version and add writing with pens. First, make a banner by slicing triangles from both ends of a rectangle shape. To find fonts that are good for writing, add text and click the "font" box. Filter the fonts for writing using the pull-down box on the right-hand side. I also like to make sure the kerned fonts box is checked here as those fonts are better for use with pens. I use Cricut fonts when working with pens generally as you will need a single line font in order for it to look like writing.

7. Once you change to a writing font, make sure the style is "writing" and the operation is "pen" in the top toolbar. It should also look correct on your screen. Remember that writing fonts will appear as a single line, but other fonts will be an outline. Be sure to click both the writing and the banner and click "attach" once you have it where you want it.

Pro Tip: You can change your pen color in a similar manner as changing the color of any object. This can help you visualize a project or use multiple pen colors in one project.

8. For this card, I just added shapes in another color, and I will add those to the front with glue, along with the banner.

9. This is a great example of a card where you can easily add writing to the inside. Just use the same procedure as above to add text with a writing font and attach it along with your score line to your card rectangle.

Note: If you add text to the inside of the other examples shown, you would need to flip those in order for the writing to be on the correct side. You can use the "flip" button in the top toolbar to do that.

10.

11.

12.

10. Click "make it" and follow the cutting basics on page 26. Remember that you can click "edit tools" if you are using the Maker with the scoring stylus to change from the scoring wheel. See installation instructions on page 14. Cut all of your paper. Design Space will prompt you when you need to change the stylus to the pen in order to draw. Follow all of the directions on the screen. Once all of your pieces are cut, you can use adhesive to assemble each of your cards. The cards with the cutouts are assembled with the second piece on the back of the front flap.

11. Have the card mat and want to make a card? Well, your process is even easier! Go to "projects" and search for the type of cards you have. In this case, I am searching "insert" but there are also other types like "cutaway." There are several different sizes, so be sure the card you pick comes in the size that you have. You can find card kits wherever Cricut products are sold.

12. Pick the card you want and then just click "make it." It really is that easy!

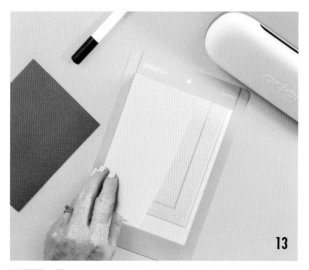

13. Peel off the liner from the Cricut card mat and add your folded card. Put the back of the card under the flap on the card mat. Push the card all the way up and all the way over to the right, then adhere the front of the card to the sticky portion of the mat.

Note: If you are using Cutaway Cards, be sure to add the backer to the card front before applying to the card mat.

14. Pick your card type as your material and make your cuts. If you have writing on the card, Design Space will prompt you to add the pen. Once the machine is done drawing, it will prompt you to add the blade back to the machine. Then it will cut your design from the front of the card. Once the card is done, just remove it from the mat. This is one place where I would use something like the spatula to remove the scrap pieces from the mat.

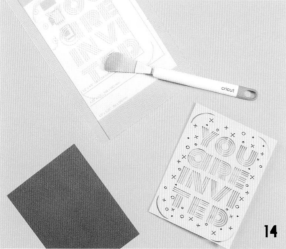

Pro Tip: When using the 2x2 Card Mat with any Explore or Maker model, be sure to move the star wheels to the center so you do not mar your material.

15. To assemble your card, just add the insert portion of the card to the cutouts on the inside of the card on all four corners. If you are using cutaway cards, you would weed away your pieces at this time. That's it! Your card is complete and ready to give. You don't even need adhesive with these types of cards.

Whatever machine you have, it is simple to make greeting cards for any occasion. Start with these simple ideas, then work your way up to more complicated designs as your skills improve.

PAPER BANNER WITH FOIL LINES

Level: Beginner

Machine requirements: Any Cricut machine

Skills: Using the foil tool

Challenge: Use the slice function skills you have already learned to add holes to your banner flag and string it on the twine instead of using the clothespins shown.

Supplies Needed

Cardstock (approximately 80 lb/216 gsm) (see Paper Types and Finishes, page 33)

Light grip (blue) Cricut mat

Fine point blade

Foil tool and foil sheets

Glue stick or other adhesive (see Paper Glue Recommendations, page 34)

Twine

Small clothespins

One thing I love making with my Cricut is party décor. It is fun to personalize it to match your theme and really celebrate in style. Let's make a simple banner for any occasion and learn to use the foil tool for adding some metallic shine to any project.

I. Add triangles in various sizes to your canvas in Cricut Design Space. You can play with the sizing here to fit your party décor. Be sure to keep in mind the size of the foil sheets you are using. If you are using the Cricut Joy, be sure to keep them within the size restrictions of that machine.

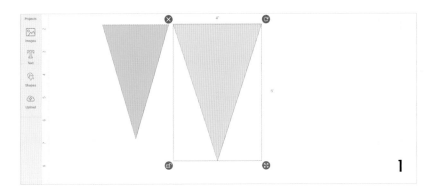

1

Note: Foiling is not available at this time on the mobile app.

(continued)

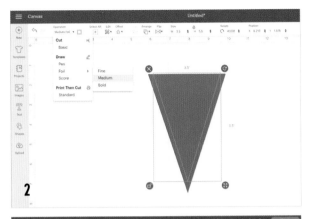

2. Change the smaller of the two triangles to a foil line using the "operation" box. I am using an Explore 3 with a medium foil tip. The Joy only has one foiling size. You can change the foil color in Design Space to get an idea of the final look of your project. Lay the foil triangle over the cut rectangle in Design Space. Pick both objects and click "attach." I did *not* want the top foil line to be on my finished project so I put it over the top of the cut line.

3. Then add text with your desired phrase and resize it to fit your flags. Be sure that each letter fits the flag before cutting.

Pro Tip: Use the advanced font menu in the top toolbar to "ungroup to letters" then move each letter over the flag to check placement and size.

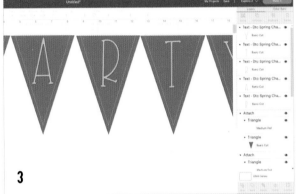

4. Cut your pieces from cardstock using the machine of your choice. See the basic cutting instructions on page 26. When Design Space prompts you for the foil, add the foil over your cardstock using the tape that comes with the foil.

5. Start by taping the foil sheet across the top. Tape the foil to your mat, gripping just a small sliver of the foil sheet.

Note: *The tape may rip your paper so you may want to test it before adding smaller pieces of foil to a large piece of paper.*

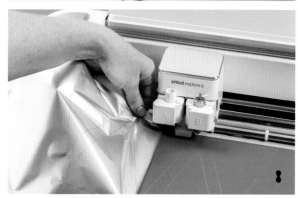

6. You will want to pull the foil as tight as you can over your cardstock and tape it down well. I like to do the top then the bottom then repeat on the sides. You can readjust as needed to remove wrinkles and tighten the sheet. Do not let your foil sheet touch the mat adhesive as it will ruin your mat. Trim the foil to size if you are using a small piece of paper.

7. Make sure your desired tip is in the foil tool. Do this by pressing the plunger on the top of the tool and look for the lines on each tip. One line is fine, two lines are medium and three lines are bold. Remove the blade and add the foil tool to that same clamp. Drop in the tool then close the clamp. The white star wheels will transfer foil to some materials.

8. When foiling is complete, Design Space will ask you to remove the foil sheet from the mat. It will NOT eject the mat completely from the machine but there will be enough hanging out for you to remove the foil sheet. Pull the foil sheet off *without* ejecting the mat from the machine. Remove carefully so you do not damage your paper. You can also save this foil sheet and utilize any unused areas of the sheet for another project.

9. Replace the foil tool with the blade, then press the "go" button to cut the flags from the cardstock. Once your pieces are cut, remove them from the mat and assemble with some adhesive. I like to start with the letter that is the widest at the bottom to get placement correct. Then use that flag as a guide for placing the letters on the remainder of the flags. To complete the banner, just clip the flags on your twine using some miniature clothespins, and you are ready to party!

CHIPBOARD CAKE TOPPER

Level: Intermediate

Machine requirements: Cricut Explore or Maker Series

Skills: Using the deep point blade, advanced text options

Challenge: If you have the Maker and the knife blade, cut thicker chipboard instead of the thinner version. You will learn more about the knife blade on page 15.

Supplies Needed

Chipboard (50 point/0.05 inch/ 1.2575 mm thick maximum for cutting with the deep point blade)

Deep point blade (Don't have the deep point blade? I have an option for you in step 3!)

Cardstock (minimum 65 lb/176 gsm) (see Paper Types and Finishes, page 33)

Medium grip (green) Cricut mat (This mat is fine for the chipboard shown here; however, you may need a strong grip mat for thicker chipboard materials)

Fine point blade

Craft knife (optional)

Glue (see Paper Glue Recommendations, page 34)

Wooden skewers

Paint, ribbon or twine (optional)

Scissors (optional)

No party would be complete without a cute cake topper to make your party décor. You can make one easily by layering a thin chipboard cut on your Cricut machine. Then decorate the front for a fun and festive addition to any cake. Have cupcakes instead? Try smaller versions of this project.

I. Add the text of your choice to Cricut Design Space and choose a font. You will want all of the letters to touch in this case to make this a one-piece cake topper. Pick the word and click "advanced" in the top toolbar, then click "ungroup to letters." You can then move each letter individually.

(continued)

2

3

2. You can also use the rotate function on individual letters so the word is more legible. Rotate using the circular arrow or type in an angle in the top toolbar. Once you have the letters the way you want them, pick all of the letters and click "weld." You will want to make sure each letter is touching another letter in order for your final design to be one piece.

3. Try different fonts to get different looks. Thicker and chunkier fonts work best. Something like the word PARTY in this example may not cut well from a thicker chipboard because of the thin lines on the T and Y. I will be using Kraft Board for this word instead as an alternate for those that do not have the deep point blade. Kraft Board is a Cricut product that is approximately a 120 lb/324 gsm cardstock and cuts with the fine point blade.

4. Duplicate your project several times to cut enough layers. The number you need depends on the thickness of your chipboard as well as how thick you want your final cake topper to be. You will also want to add one that is for cutting from the paper of your choice that will go on top. Click "make it" to cut your design. You may need to change the material size on the next screen, as the chipboard does not often come in 12 x 12–inch (30.5 x 30.5–cm) sheets. Changing the material size will ensure everything will fit once you start cutting.

5. Cut the chipboard as well as the paper using your Cricut machine and the basic cutting instructions on page 26. For the chipboard, I used the corrugated cardboard setting then clicked "edit tools" and picked the deep point blade. As noted, you can use Kraft Board to cut all of your layers and just use the fine point blade. You will also want to move the star wheels all the way over to the right for any chipboard. They tend to drag on thicker materials and can cause your cuts to be off.

5

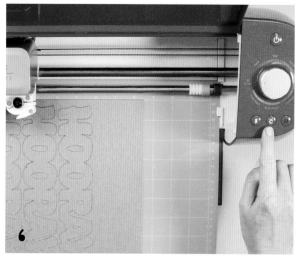

6. Once the first pass is done, do not eject the mat. Instead, lift your material to see if it is cut through. If it is not cut through, click the "go" button on your machine for another pass. Repeat for each cut. Chipboard is inconsistent from each supplier, so I find this is the best way to cut it. Generally, I find that five to six passes will cut 50 pt chipboard. You can use this same method for a thinner chipboard as long as you check your cuts in between passes. Once the material is cut through, eject the mat and remove the cut pieces from the scrap. The edges may be rough. I generally clean them up with a craft knife.

7. I cut the word HOORAY from a Cricut product called Kraft Board. I had to do 6 layers of it as compared to just 2 of the chipboard. However, it does use the fine point blade to cut, so it is a great option if you don't have the deep point blade. Assemble your cake topper by adding glue in between layers and stacking them. Align each layer with the layer below it.

8. You will also want to glue a wooden skewer to the back. Want your cake topper to look finished from the back as well as the front? Cut a second cardstock piece but flip the image before cutting. Then glue that piece on the back to cover up your wooden skewer.

9. Allow the glue to dry then add the cake topper to your cake. I like to allow mine to dry with something heavy on top so that it doesn't curl. If you don't like the raw edges of the chipboard, feel free to paint them before adding your cardstock, or you can cover them with ribbon or twine. Trim the wooden skewer with scissors if you need your cake topper to be shorter.

GIFT BOX AND BOW

Level: Beginner

Machine requirements: Cricut Explore or Maker Series

Skills: Uploading a file, using the deboss tip (for Maker only)

Challenge: Mix and match projects from this book by making a few paper flowers (see Framed Flower Shadow Box, page 79) for the top of a gift box.

Supplies Needed

Kraft Board (This is made by Cricut and is my personal favorite for making boxes. It is equivalent to a 120 lb/324 gsm cardstock.)

Fine point blade

Cardstock (65 lb/176 gsm for bows, 80 lb/216 gsm for debossing) (see Paper Types and Finishes, page 33)

Light grip (blue) Cricut mat

Strong permanent adhesive (see Paper Glue Recommendations, page 34)

Deboss tip with QuickSwap housing (only for Maker and debossed version on page 14)

Looking to give a small gift? Why not make a gift box with your Cricut machine? This project is a great way to customize your gifts with a handmade gift box. Add the bow or debossed heart as shown, or come up with another way to decorate your box that is all your own. Be sure to customize this project for your gift recipient by using colors and embellishments that they will love.

1. First, you will need the file that is going to be used for this project. You can find all files used in this book at cricuthandbook.com. You can see more about file types and working with ZIP files on page 31. Click "upload" on the left toolbar in Cricut Design Space. Click "upload image."

1

(continued)

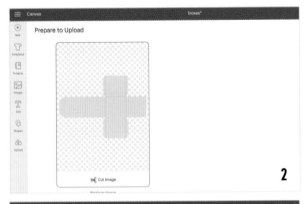

2. Then click "browse" and find the file for the box on your device. Remember that on PC computers, SVG files may appear as HTML files. You will also need to unzip any files before starting the upload process. You should see the file on the next screen; then click the "upload" button to finish.

3. Highlight what you just uploaded in the recent uploads section and click "add to canvas." Resize if needed once it is on your canvas.

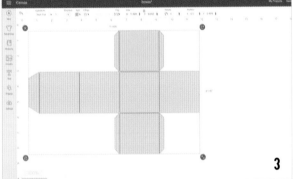

4. All lines on the file will upload as cut lines. Pick the layer with the fold lines and change the line type to "score" using the operation box in the top toolbar. Then pick both layers and click "attach."

5. Use the skills you have learned in previous projects to cut and score the Kraft Board for the box (see the Chipboard Cake Topper on page 51).

6. Practice uploading files by adding a bow to your project as well. You will find the file for the bow in the same location. The bow can be cut from regular cardstock.

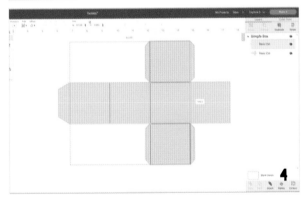

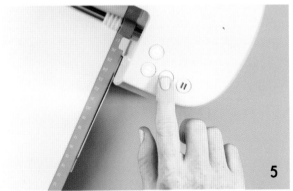

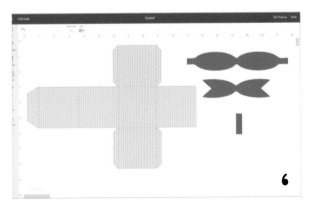

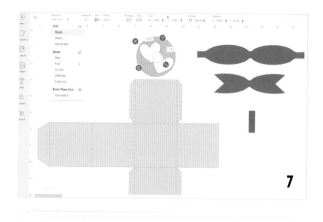

7. Have the Maker and want to add more embellishments to your box? I love using the deboss tool to add something special to paper crafts. I made a simple circle with two hearts inside. Pick each heart and change those to deboss lines in the operation box in the top toolbar. Remember this option will only appear if you have the Maker or Maker 3 picked as your machine.

8. Pick the circle as well as both hearts and click "attach." The machine will prompt you to add your deboss tool as well as when it is time to change to the fine point blade for cutting. You will add the deboss tip to the QuickSwap housing before putting it in your Maker.

9. Once all of your pieces are cut, start assembling the gift box. Fold on all score lines and add adhesive to the flaps on each side piece. Don't add adhesive to the flap at the top.

10. Fold the box and secure the adhesive; then you can place your gift inside.

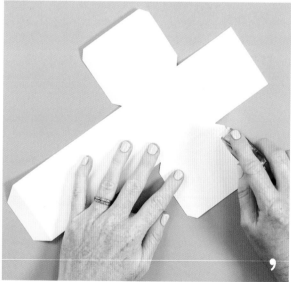

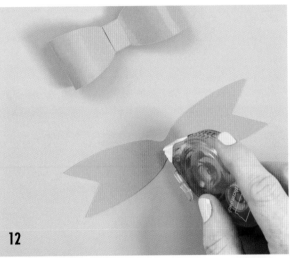

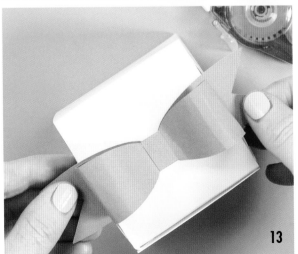

11. The first option for adding embellishments to your box is to make the paper bow for the outside. Fold the long piece of the bow to where the two ends are touching the middle. Add adhesive to hold it together.

12. Wrap the smallest piece around the center and use adhesive to secure. Then secure your assembled piece to the bottom of the bow with adhesive.

13. Add the bow to the top of your box with a little adhesive. You can also cut a straight strip of cardstock to wrap around your box.

14. The second option is to add the debossed embellishment to the top of the box with some adhesive. I think this is a more elegant option and really works for wedding favors and bridal showers. Here I used a foam adhesive to add some dimension to the final product.

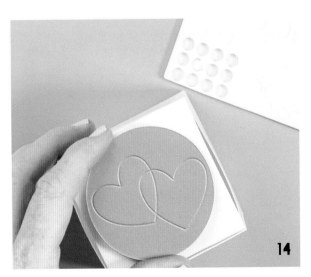

Now that you are feeling confident with paper crafts, it is time to add another material to your Cricut crafting. For the purpose of this book, vinyl is a sticky adhesive-backed sheet or roll. Once you cut it on your Cricut, it can be placed, much like a sticker, on non-porous or hard surfaces. This material will cut on any Cricut machine with a fine point blade, so these projects are great for beginners.

Note: *If you purchased some vinyl and it is NOT sticky on the back, refer to page 85, as you most likely have Heat Transfer Vinyl (HTV) or Iron-On instead.*

VINYL CRAFTING BASICS

PERMANENT VERSUS REMOVABLE

The first thing you need to consider is if your project needs permanent or removable vinyl. Here are a few things to consider:

- Permanent vinyl has a strong adhesive, allowing it to last longer, especially outdoors or in applications where it will get used frequently. A sealer may still be required for this product to be completely permanent; however, I recommend it for most applications.

Pro Tip: *The adhesive on permanent vinyl needs to sit for 72 hours after application before use in order to get maximum adhesion.*

- Removable vinyl is easier to remove as the adhesive is not as strong. That makes it perfect for temporary applications like wall decals, seasonal signs or party decorations. It still may not be easy to remove from your surface and it could leave a residue. Most vinyl packaging states how long the vinyl is considered to be removable, so keep that in mind when adding it to any surface.

Adhesive vinyl of either type can be removed from your surface with enough effort. Use the tips above to pick the best option for your project and follow all instructions that come with your brand for the best results.

VINYL BRANDS AND TYPES

There are many brands and types of vinyl on the market. Let's start with the different types:

- Glossy: As a general rule, permanent vinyl will be glossy.

- Matte: In most brands, removable vinyl will have a matte finish.

- Window cling: These are perfect for adding temporary designs to windows.

- Stencil vinyl: For more on this topic, see Stenciling Basics (page 135).

- Smart Vinyl: This material can be used without a mat on the Cricut Joy, Explore 3 and Maker 3 only. The Smart Vinyl for the Cricut Joy is a smaller width than the version for the Explore 3 and Maker 3.

(continued)

- **Glitter:** Add some sparkle to your projects with glitter vinyl.

- **Shimmer:** This one has a shimmer without having actual glitter.

- **Mosaic:** This one comes with shapes pre-cut out of it in patterns.

- **Metallic:** If you are looking for a metallic finish, choose from a wide variety of vinyl with a metal look.

- **Foil:** This product gives a metallic look, almost as if you laid a sheet of colored foil over your surface.

- **Patterned or printed:** This vinyl comes preprinted with a variety of designs and/or characters.

- **Printable:** Print your own vinyl with your home printer and cut it on your Cricut. See Print Then Cut (page 153).

- **Holographic:** This vinyl shines and almost appears to change colors as it moves.

Now that you have decided which type will work best for your project, you might be asking which brands work best. I do find a BIG difference between different brands of vinyl. I tend to stick with name brands like Cricut, Oracal or Siser for most of my projects. I find that these brands generally cut, weed and stick better than off-brands. That said, there are some off-brands on the market that are amazing. You can definitely shop around; however, I would buy one sheet or one roll to test before investing too much into vinyl you have never used.

TRANSFER TAPE BRANDS AND TYPES

Transfer tape is what you will use to move your vinyl from the backing paper to your project. This tape is what keeps your pieces in place as you transfer the design. There are two main types of transfer tape that you will need in your crafting:

- **Regular:** You will use this most often, as most vinyl products will transfer with a regular grip transfer tape. If you need a lighter tack for adding vinyl to paper, use a regular grip and stick it to your shirt a few times before using.

- **Strong Grip:** This is only really used for glitter vinyl and a few other specialty products. You DO NOT want to use it with regular vinyl, as you will never get your vinyl off of the tape. It really is that strong! However, glitter vinyl cannot be used with regular transfer tape, as the tape will not pick it up.

As far as brands, I have tried many of them and I really think it comes down to personal preference and what works best with your particular brand of vinyl. I tend to stick to name-brand transfer tapes; however, I have used a variety of off-brands with success. The only issue I see with some off-brands is that they will leave a residue on the vinyl if left for extended periods. So if you are selling your decals, you may want to test your transfer tape before shipping it to your customer.

Pro Tip: Transfer tape can be used more than one time. Reuse a piece of transfer tape several times while you are crafting. When it stops working, toss it and get another piece.

With transfer tape, you will see some different options and, again, this comes down to personal preference.

- **Gridlines:** I personally love transfer tape with gridlines as it helps me to align the vinyl and keep it straight.

- **Clear tape:** This tape is super clear but doesn't have any gridlines.

- **Frosted tape:** Some transfer tape almost has a frosted finish but it is clear enough to see your design through.

- **Paper tape:** This is like masking tape on a large roll and is very difficult to see through. Some people prefer it but I generally do not use this type of transfer tape.

Note: *Not all transfer tapes can withstand heat. The next chapter will dive into heat applications; see Heat Transfer Mask (page 86).*

WEEDING EXPLAINED

You may have heard the term "weeding" in reference to vinyl or crafting in general, which is the removal of all excess vinyl from your project. In other words: everything that you don't want transferred to your surface. This includes everything around the outside as well as things like the centers of letters or designs. It is similar to weeding your garden of anything you do not want.

The items you weed away from your design will be thrown away and scrapped. If you want to save scrap pieces from your sheet, be sure to trim those away with scissors before weeding. See Vinyl on a Tumbler (page 77) for an easy way to use scraps.

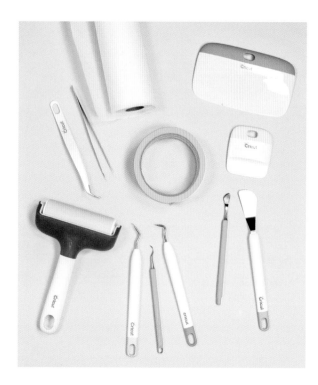

VINYL TOOLS TO CONSIDER

There are certain tools that you will probably want to have when you dive into vinyl. You can see more details about beginner tools on page 20, but here is a brief list of supplies to keep on hand:

- Weeding tools
- Scraper
- Tweezers
- Parchment paper
- Brayer
- Painter's tape

CUT SETTINGS FOR VINYL

While all vinyl cuts with the fine point blade, there is a wide variety of setting options to choose from. Vinyl should be cut with what is called a "kiss cut," which means that the vinyl itself is cut but the backing paper underneath should remain uncut. I usually start with the cut setting that most represents the type of vinyl that I am cutting. I recommend always doing a small test cut when using a material for the first time with that machine or after changing a blade to double-check the cut setting works.

I recommend making notes when you get a setting figured out for a particular brand of vinyl. Remember that the cut settings in Design Space are set using the Cricut brand of materials, so you will need to experiment when choosing another material brand or type.

Note: *For the Oracal brand of vinyl, 651 is permanent and 631 is removable. These terms can be confusing when you are looking to buy vinyl for the first time.*

HOW TO PUT VINYL ON THE MAT

Vinyl is placed with the good side up on the mat. Generally, a light grip mat will work for most vinyl types. If you have any issues with a certain brand or type not wanting to stick, feel free to try the green standard grip mat. I often use it for things like glitter vinyl or vinyl that is curled tightly and will not lay down. As always, press the vinyl down well and make sure it is not lifting anywhere.

VINYL TROUBLESHOOTING

Having issues with your vinyl? Try the tips below for application and cutting.

- If your vinyl is not cutting correctly, check the stickiness of your mat and the condition of your blade. Clean your mat and/or blade and try cutting again.

- Many issues are often fixed by using a different brand of vinyl. Some generic brands are inexpensive but also poorly made.

- Intricate or fine details not cutting correctly? Try the washi tape cut setting. This setting goes slower and not as deep. However, you will probably need to cut your material twice when using this setting. Cut the material once, then, before ejecting the mat from the machine, click the "go" button on the machine again. This will cut another pass over your project. WARNING: Do not try to do this if you unloaded your mat as it will not line up exactly. You can also consider making your design larger or removing some of the smaller details to get a better cut.

(continued)

- If the vinyl does not cut all the way through, try choosing a thicker vinyl setting like glitter or chalkboard vinyl. If the Cricut cuts all the way through the backing, play with settings that are for thinner vinyl types. You can also use the "more" and "less" pressure settings (page 27).

- Having issues weeding? Your vinyl may not be cut correctly. A cut that is too shallow or too deep can cause issues.

- If your vinyl is not sticking to the transfer tape, try burnishing down more from the front and the back. Occasionally I have to run a hair dryer over the back of my vinyl to get it to release.

- The vinyl should stick to your surface when applied. If it does not, you may need to check your surface type for compatibility or switch brands of vinyl.

- Can't remove the transfer tape? Check the bullet above for adhesion issues, then see Transfer Tape Brands and Types (page 62) and make sure you have the right transfer tape. If all of that is correct, burnish the surface more and peel back slowly at a sharp angle. You may also try changing transfer tape brands.

- If your vinyl is lifting from the surface after application, be sure to press it down well with the scraper or your fingers. You will also want to wait at least 72 hours after application before use for maximum adhesion.

- Remember that test cuts are always a good idea if you have a new brand of vinyl or if you change blades in your machine.

BEYOND THE BASICS

Are you ready to expand your vinyl knowledge? There is so much you can do with this material.

- Layering: Although there are certain types of vinyl that cannot be layered (for instance glitter can only be a top layer), the majority of vinyl types can be put one on top of another. You can see one hack in Wood Sign with Vinyl (page 72).

- Sealing: I mentioned that permanent vinyl does last a long time; however, it can still be removed. There are a few sealing options that you can use for more longevity. You can see an example of sealing vinyl in Wood Sign with Vinyl (page 72).

- Application hacks: If you are struggling with applying vinyl straight or in the correct location, try the hack found in Framed Flower Shadow Box (page 79) to help.

- Print your own designs at home: See Print Then Cut Stickers (page 159) for more on printable vinyl and a project using it.

Now that you have some information about vinyl, it is time to start crafting with it! Work your way through the projects in this chapter to learn more about vinyl and how to use it in your craft projects.

PANTRY LABELS

Level: Beginner

Machine requirements: Any Cricut machine

Skills: Using transfer tape, weeding vinyl and color sync

Challenge: Expand your skills with the other projects in this chapter, then come back to this project and make more complicated labels with additional colors or covering larger areas.

Supplies Needed

Permanent adhesive vinyl (in the color of your choice)

Fine point blade

Light grip (blue) Cricut mat

Weeding tools

Transfer tape

Scraper

Containers for labeling

One thing that I think everyone loves to make with their Cricut is labels. It is a great way to organize your home easily with just your Cricut and some vinyl. You will be labeling so much more than just the items in your pantry after you become an expert at vinyl crafting. Remember to stick to hard surfaces when working with vinyl for the best results.

I. In Design Space, add text in the font of your choice and resize to work with your containers. If you would like to add a little something to your pantry labels, add two rectangles to your canvas and resize. You want the inside one to fit around your text. Pick both rectangles and click "align" in the top toolbar then "center."

Pro Tip: Use a sewing tape measure to get accurate measurements on rounded surfaces.

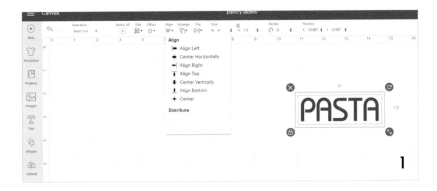

(continued)

YEAST

BEANS

PASTA

RICE

2

3

2. With both rectangles picked, click on "slice" in the bottom right toolbar. Then delete everything except for the outline portion. Repeat for as many labels as you will be making. For each label, pick both the outline and the text and align to the center. Then pick everything on the canvas and click "color sync" in the right toolbar. Drag the white layers to black in this case.

3. This is a quick and easy way to make all of the items on your canvas one color. Then choose each word and outline and click "attach" to cut them as one piece. Resize as needed to fit your containers. Then click "make it" and follow the basic cutting instructions on page 26. Add the vinyl to the mat (see How to Put Vinyl on the Mat, page 65) and pick a vinyl setting in Design Space. Remember to pick a setting that is closest to the type of vinyl that you are cutting. Then cut your material with the fine point blade.

4. Weed away all the excess vinyl. I like to start with a weeding tool in one corner and start pulling back all of the excess around the outside.

5. Then use your weeding tool to remove the centers of the letters as well as the center of the design. Discard all of these pieces.

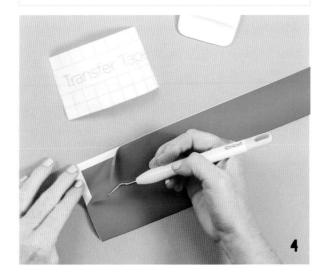

4

5

6. Now it is time to apply your design. Be sure to clean your surface well by wiping it off or cleaning it with rubbing alcohol. Then cut a piece of transfer tape a little larger than your label and stick it on the front of your design.

7. Burnish the transfer tape from the front with your scraper. Burnishing is just rubbing the surface with the tool while pressing down. Flip the vinyl over and burnish from the back as well.

8. Then peel the backing paper from the back of the vinyl. The easiest way to do this is to pull at a sharp angle so that it is almost touching itself. You want to leave the vinyl on the tape. Go slowly and make sure you get all of the pieces. If the pieces do not want to stick, lay the backing paper back down and burnish more before trying again. Occasionally, I need to heat the backing paper with a hair dryer to get it to release.

9. Once your vinyl is on your transfer tape, it is time to apply it to your surface. You can use a ruler to place your design or just eyeball it.

10. Once the vinyl is on the surface, burnish it well, then start peeling back the transfer tape. The vinyl should remain on your containers. If it doesn't, put the transfer tape back down and burnish more before trying again.

11. Now that your vinyl is on your container, burnish lightly with your fingers to make sure it is stuck all the way down. Then wait 72 hours before use for maximum adhesion. Repeat with the remaining containers.

Pro Tip: You can reuse the same piece of transfer tape for several containers if you cut it to the size of your largest label. Discard only when you are done with the project or it is no longer sticky.

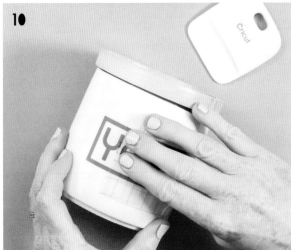

WOOD SIGN WITH VINYL

Level: Beginner

Machine requirements: Any Cricut machine

Skills: Layering vinyl, sealing options

Challenge: Design a sign of your very own using text and shapes from previous lessons; then make a second version!

Supplies Needed

Permanent adhesive vinyl (in the colors of your choice; glitter vinyl can only be used as the top layer, as vinyl will not stick well on top of it)

Fine point blade

Light grip (blue) Cricut mat

Weeding tools

Transfer tape

Scraper

Parchment paper

Wood surface (painted or unpainted)

Sealer and paintbrush (optional)

Make a personalized sign for your home with these techniques. The layered vinyl technique shown here is useful any time you want to make a design with more than one color of vinyl. Start simple with this sign, then expand to more complicated projects as your skills increase.

I. Upload the SVG file found at cricuthandbook.com to Design Space for cutting the design shown, using the instructions on page 55. Resize to fit your particular sign blank. Keep in mind the size restrictions of your machine and the mat sizes that you have on hand. Then click "make it" and follow the basic cutting instructions on page 26.

Pro Tip: *For rolls of vinyl, you can leave the excess hanging off the edge of the mat when cutting. There is no need to trim the roll before cutting.*

(continued)

2. Once cut, you will need to weed each color. Remove everything around the outside as well as things like the centers of letters.

3. Now it is time to layer the vinyl. Cut a piece of transfer tape large enough to fit over your entire design. Start with the topmost layer and apply the transfer tape with the design in the center. Burnish it down well and remove the backing paper.

4. Then add parchment paper over your second layer, leaving a small strip of the backing paper exposed.

5. The vinyl and transfer tape of your first layer will not stick to the parchment paper. Locate the first layer on top of the second, making sure everything is lined up.

6. Then stick the transfer tape to that small strip of exposed backing paper from the second layer. Pull out the parchment paper slowly, pressing the vinyl down as you go.

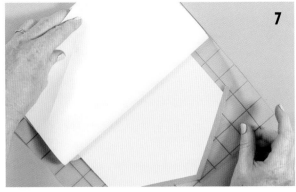

7. Burnish down well and remove the backing paper from the second layer. Repeat for each layer. You want to work from the top to the bottom. You should be left with the entire design on your transfer tape and ready for your surface.

8. You can use the parchment paper to help you align the design on your surface as well. Use the same method to make sure the vinyl is in location before pulling out the parchment paper and adhering your design.

9. Burnish down well and then remove the transfer tape.

Note: For any painted wood surface, allow your paint to cure for at least 24 hours before applying the vinyl to ensure that your paint does not lift up with the transfer tape. I also recommend a water-based paint for your surface.

10. Once the transfer tape has been removed, burnish down the vinyl well. For indoor use, the sign can be used with just the vinyl in place.

11. If you want to use your sign outdoors, a sealer will help the vinyl to last longer. My personal favorite is Minwax® Polycrylic™. Allow the vinyl to cure for 72 hours before applying any sealer. Then apply three coats of sealer, allowing it to dry for 2 hours between coats. I apply over the entire sign, not just the vinyl, for a consistent appearance.

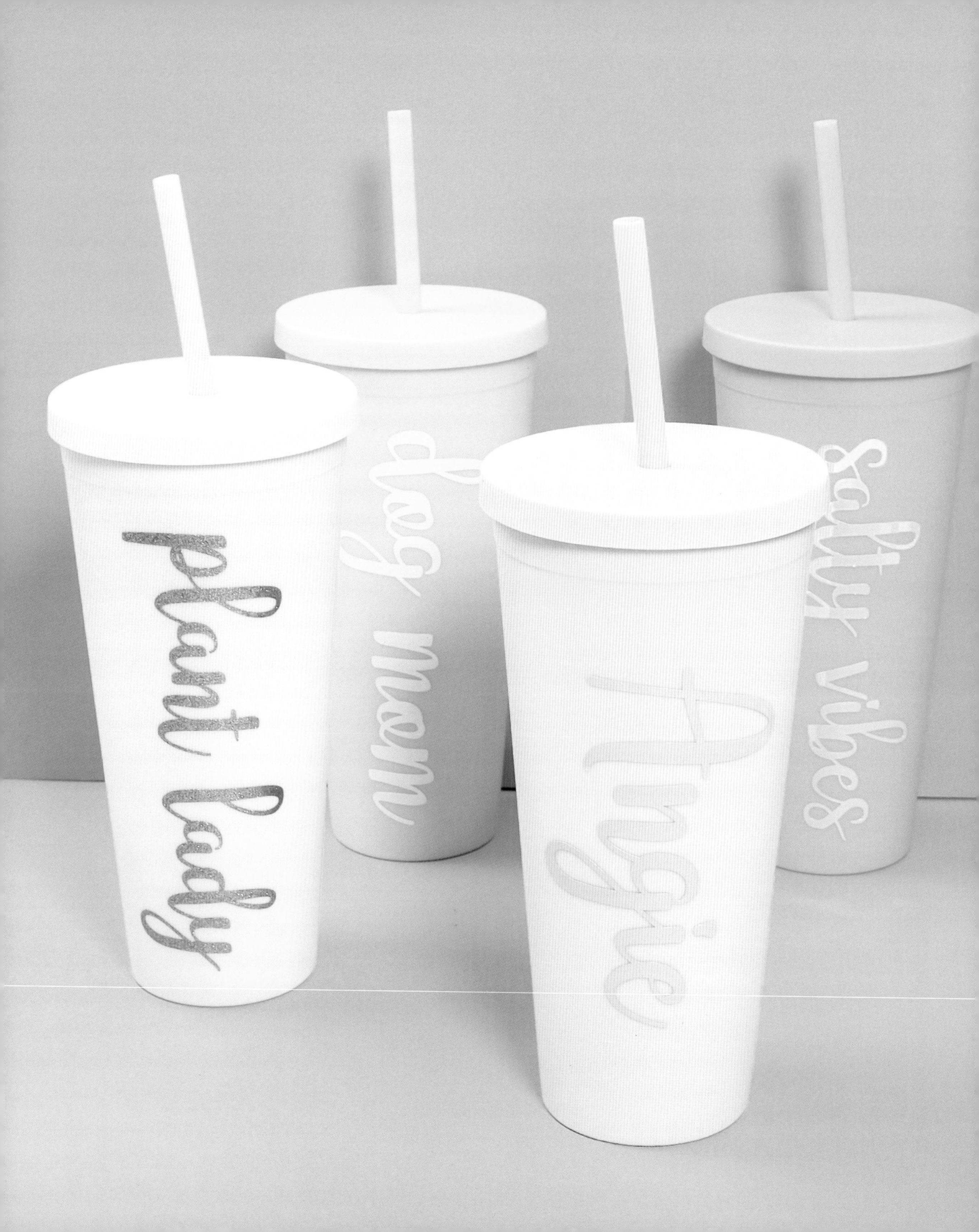
plant lady
dog mom
Angie
salty vibes

VINYL ON A TUMBLER

Level: Beginner

Machine requirements: Any Cricut machine

Skills: Letter spacing, using scraps, moving cuts on the mat

Challenge: Add several images or words to one tumbler for an all-over design that is all your own.

Supplies Needed

Permanent adhesive vinyl (in the color of your choice)

Fine point blade

Light grip (blue) Cricut mat

Weeding tools

Transfer tape

Scraper

Tumbler (Be sure to choose a tumbler with a hard surface like plastic, metal or even glass. Vinyl does not work well on surfaces like silicone.)

Need to drink more water? Looking for a gift to give a friend? A personalized tumbler is the answer! Make a tumbler with the words or name of your choice using this tutorial and your favorite vinyl. This is also a great way to use up those smaller scrap pieces you have from other projects.

1. Add text to your Design Space canvas in your chosen font. Adjust the letter spacing in the top toolbar until all of the letters touch. Once done, pick the entire word and click "weld" in the bottom right toolbar. Repeat for as many tumblers as needed (I am making several different ones).

2. Make all of your words the same color on your canvas and click "make it." On the next screen, click each design and move it around on your mat, using the gridlines on this screen to align the words.

(continued)

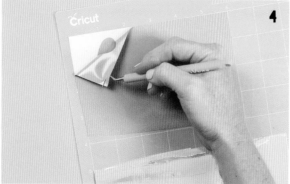

3. Be sure to move the designs in Design Space to the same location of the vinyl that is on your actual mat. You will also need to keep the scrap pieces larger than your designs to allow for some error in placement.

Pro Tip: If you are using the app on an iPhone or iPad, you can use the SnapMat feature to take a picture of the mat for better placement.

4. Cut the vinyl on your Cricut machine using the instructions on page 64. Be sure to pick the cut setting for the type of vinyl you are using. When using multiple types, pick the setting for the thickest vinyl you have on the mat. Then use weeding tools to weed away all of your excess vinyl. Weeding small pieces of vinyl is often easier if you leave them on the mat. That holds them still while weeding and keeps them flat.

5. Apply transfer tape to your vinyl and burnish down well. Then peel away the backing paper. Apply your design to the tumbler and burnish down well, then peel back the transfer tape.

6. Press the vinyl down well on your surface and allow it to cure for 72 hours before use. I find that a regular sealer on this type of project does not extend the life of the cup. You can hand wash to make your tumbler last longer. However, I have used my dishwasher for projects with just permanent vinyl and no sealer without issue. For the ultimate in protection, you can use a two-part epoxy coating over certain tumblers. Epoxy coatings are an advanced technique, so be sure to research best practices.

FRAMED FLOWER SHADOW BOX

Level: Intermediate

Machine requirements: Any Cricut machine

Skills: Strong grip transfer tape, hinge method

Challenge: Complete another shadow box, but this time use a layered vinyl design on the front.

This project is a great way to mix and match the materials that we have used so far. Combine paper and vinyl into one gorgeous piece of art for your home or to give as a gift to someone special. Personalize this project with the colors and finishes of your choice.

1. For the flowers, use the skills you learned on page 55 to upload the SVG file to Cricut Design Space. Resize the file to your desired size. You can make these flowers large or small. I find that four to a sheet of paper is a good size for most shadowboxes.

Supplies Needed

Glitter adhesive vinyl (in the color of your choice)

Cardstock (65 lb/176 gsm) (see Paper Types and Finishes, page 33)

Fine point blade

Standard grip (green) or light grip (blue) Cricut mat (you may find your vinyl needs the standard grip)

Hot glue and glue gun

Hot glue fingertips (optional)

Shadow box

Weeding tools

Strong grip transfer tape (check the brand of vinyl you are using and make sure this is required)

Scraper

Painter's tape

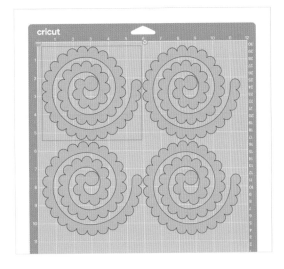

1

(continued)

2

2. Then pick the quote of your choice and use the text function to add that to your canvas as well. Type the quote and use the "ungroup to lines" button under "advanced" in the top toolbar to separate the words so you can move them around. I like drawing a box the size I want my design to be and laying out the words in Design Space to fit.

3. Next, delete the box, pick all of the words and click "attach." Then click "make it" and use the basic cutting instructions on page 26. I like having one mat with my quote and just one mat of flowers. You can cut any mat as many times as you would like just by clicking on it. Cut cardstock for the flowers and glitter vinyl for the quote. Remember to pick the glitter vinyl setting for your vinyl cuts.

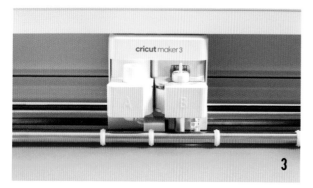

3

4. First, assemble all of your flowers. For this 8 x 10–inch (20.3 x 25–cm) shadowbox, I used 30 flowers. You can use as many as you would like depending on how large you make each flower and how tightly you add them to the box. For each flower, start on the outside end and start rolling tightly.

5. Continue to tightly roll the flower toward the center. Once you get to the center, you will have a large circle that is for the bottom of the flower.

Note: I like using my fingers for rolling flowers, but there are also several tools on the market you can try as well.

4

5

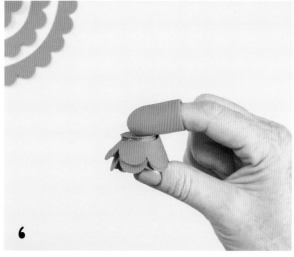

6. I like to slowly release my fingers to allow the flower to expand. Once you are happy with the look and size, flip the flower over and add hot glue to that circle. Place the circle with the hot glue onto the bottom of the flower. Then hold the flower tightly as the glue cools. This is where some hot glue fingertips come in handy. The flower may require some extra glue on the back as well.

7. You can form some of the outer petals with your fingers if desired to create a fuller look. Once you have all of your flowers assembled, add a piece of cardstock to the back of your shadowbox.

8. Then lay the flowers into location. Use hot glue on the back of each one to secure into place.

9. Now you can work on the front design. Weed your glitter vinyl, removing all excess from around the outside as well as the centers of letters. Here I used a craft knife to go around my design while it was still on the mat to waste as little of this sheet as possible. Once weeded, apply the strong grip transfer tape to your glitter vinyl and burnish down well. You want to burnish from the front and the back.

10. Then put your vinyl in location on your shadow-box with the backing paper still attached. This allows you to move the design around and get it in an exact location before sticking it down. Use painter's tape to secure the vinyl down the center.

11. Then peel away the backing paper on one side. Trim the backing paper on that side with a pair of scissors and burnish the design down well with a scraper.

12. Then remove the painter's tape from the middle and remove the backing paper on the opposite side. Burnish the entire design down well then remove the transfer tape.

13. Finally, assemble your shadowbox and enjoy it in any room of your home!

HTV

There is another version of vinyl that you are going to love! Heat Transfer Vinyl (HTV) or "Iron-On" vinyl has a heat-activated adhesive and is used mostly on fabric crafts and other porous surfaces. There are many types, brands and styles that will work with the projects you have in mind. Like the adhesive vinyl from the previous chapter, you can cut this on any Cricut machine with the fine point blade. That makes it perfect for beginners!

HTV CRAFTING BASICS

WHAT MAKES HTV DIFFERENT FROM REGULAR VINYL?

Well, a few things actually. First of all, the type of adhesive is different. Think of it this way: if you used regular adhesive vinyl on your shirt, it would be like putting a sticker on yourself. It would be temporary and would not be able to be washed. That is where HTV comes in! This special vinyl product has an adhesive that activates with heat and bonds to your fabric. That means you can make designs on your shirt that will last!

There is another really important difference. HTV already has the carrier sheet attached to it. As a general rule, you don't need any other transfer tape or masking. Now, there are always exceptions to the rule, and we will get into those in a bit. For now, remember this also means you will need to mirror your design when cutting and put the HTV on the mat in a very specific way. Be sure to keep reading for details!

HOW CAN YOU TELL THE DIFFERENCE?

Maybe you have a pile of "vinyl" from a friend and you are wondering whether it is HTV or adhesive vinyl. How do you tell the difference once it is out of the packaging? My top recommendation is to peel back the corner of the sheet and see if it is sticky or not. If it is sticky, it is adhesive vinyl. If it is not sticky, it is HTV. Remember that the clear carrier sheet of HTV will be sticky but the actual product will not be.

HTV BRANDS AND TYPES

Just like vinyl, there are a ton of possibilities with this craft medium. You can experiment with all of these or pick a couple of favorites.

- Regular: Generally you will use a standard (regular) HTV for most projects.

- Glitter: It adds that sparkle to shirts, tote bags and so much more.

- Smart Iron-On: This material can be used without a mat on the Cricut Joy, Explore 3 and Maker 3 only. Remember that the size for the Joy is different from the size for the Explore 3 and Maker 3.

- Patterned or printed: This HTV comes preprinted with a variety of designs and/or characters. With printed HTV, you will often find that you need to purchase a separate mask that will be like transfer tape used for vinyl.

- Foil: You can add a metallic shine with this HTV.

- Mosaic: It comes with shapes pre-cut out of it in patterns.

- Printable: Print your own HTV designs from any home printer. I find that printable HTV is a more durable product than t-shirt transfers.

- **Holographic:** It shines and almost appears to change colors as it moves.

- **Flex:** This specialty type is for applying to things like workout clothes where you need the HTV to stretch with the fabric.

- **Glow in the dark:** This is perfect for adding some Halloween fun to your projects!

- **Puff:** This material puffs up once applied and almost looks like puff paint on the surface.

- **Flocked:** Don't want as much puff? This material is raised and fuzzy once applied.

- **Reflective:** This is handy for adding designs to running gear.

There are also many, many brands on the market you can choose from. I tend to stick with name brands like Cricut and Siser; however, there are several other great ones. I always test a new brand on a project for myself and make sure it holds up through some laundry cycles before using it to make things for others.

HEAT TRANSFER MASK

Adhesive vinyl has to have a separate transfer tape for application. HTV, however, generally comes with a mask attached for application. There are some patterned or printed HTV brands that do require the separate purchase of a mask. When purchasing these types, be sure to check the listing to see if you will need a heat transfer mask. If you do, I recommend purchasing the same brand as the HTV.

Note: *This masking is special and heat resistant. You cannot just use transfer tape that is intended for adhesive vinyl. It will melt and you will be left with a mess!*

Products that require separate masking also require different instructions for cutting as well as application. I recommend carefully reading the instructions on the website of the brand you purchase.

Pro Tip: *In a pinch, you can use the carrier sheet from another HTV project for your patterned HTV.*

HTV TOOLS

You may have used some of these tools with the vinyl projects in the previous chapter but it is worth mentioning them again. You can see more details about beginner tools on page 20.

- Weeding tools

- Scraper

- Tweezers

- Brayer

- Teflon sheet or parchment paper

- Light box (I find this is really useful for HTV but it is not required.)

For HTV, you will also need a heat source, as the adhesive is heat-activated. See Heat Sources and Accessories (page 21) to compare the different options and choose the one that will work for you.

If you are using an iron or handheld press, make sure you have a solid surface (like a solid table or even the floor). Don't use your ironing board, as it flexes away from you when you add pressure. I also recommend placing something under your project, as you don't want to damage your surface with the heat. You can use a folded towel for this purpose or a heat mat. You can read more about these options on page 22.

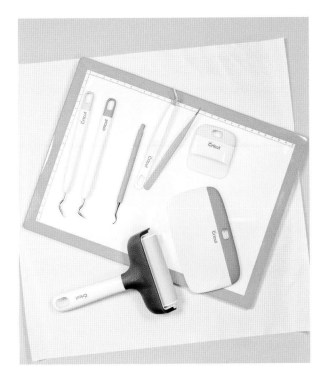

BLANK TYPES AND MATERIALS

HTV can be applied to a wide variety of materials. I have used shirts and other clothing made of everything from cotton to polyester to silk. You want to make sure the brand of HTV that you are using is good on the surface you want to apply it to. Also, if you are applying to a material that is stretchy, be sure to buy an HTV that will flex with the material.

HTV can be used on so much more than shirts! It is great on fabric surfaces, but I also like to use it on wood and cork. If you have a porous surface, chances are you can get HTV to work on it! Now, these odd blank types usually require some trial and error, so be prepared for that. However, I think you will love the results that HTV will give you.

PREPPING YOUR BLANK

Moisture can be the enemy of HTV! I like to run my iron or press over my fabric before adding HTV. This removes moisture from the fabric and increases the permanence of the adhesive to the surface. Most brands have preheating as a required step, so make sure you're following the directions.

Many shirts you buy at the craft store are ready to go as soon as you get them home. You can start adding HTV as soon as you peel off the label. These shirts are often pre-shrunk as well which means they will not shrink in the wash and wrinkle up your HTV designs. Look for labels that indicate pre-shrunk materials for crafting.

Other times, you will have a hard time getting your HTV to stick. I find that places like department stores will often have a coating on their shirts (to make them feel soft) that repels the adhesive of HTV. Generally, washing will get rid of that residue and you can continue with the project as normal. Occasionally, I will find a shirt that I just cannot get to work. If you wash before application, be sure not to use fabric softener, as that can hinder the ability of the HTV to stick.

CUT SETTINGS FOR HTV

As with vinyl, you can choose from a wide variety of settings in Cricut Design Space. Again, you want to cut the material with a "kiss cut" so that only the HTV is cut and not the clear carrier sheet. Start with a cut setting that is closest to the material you are using and do a test cut if you need to. From there, you can choose a thicker setting or a thinner setting. All settings in Design Space will be under "Iron-On", as that is the Cricut designation for HTV.

Important: *You will want to mirror your cut in Cricut Design Space when cutting HTV. This applies to almost every type of HTV except any that require a separate mask. The rule of thumb is if the GOOD side is down on the mat, you want to mirror your design.*

HOW TO PUT HTV ON THE MAT

You always want to put the carrier sheet of your HTV down on the mat. That is generally the shiny side, as the carrier sheet itself is a clear plastic film. This means that you will be mirroring your cut in these cases. The ONLY time you need to break this rule is if the specific HTV you are using has different instructions. This generally happens with printed HTV, as the cutting and application process can be different from other brands.

A light grip mat will work for most HTV. If you have any issues with a certain brand or type not wanting to stick, feel free to try the green standard grip mat. Some HTV products can be curled off of the roll and will require the extra strength. I also find that the carrier sheets on some brands don't like to stick to the adhesive. I have even used a strong grip mat for some of those. As always, press the HTV down and make sure it is stuck well.

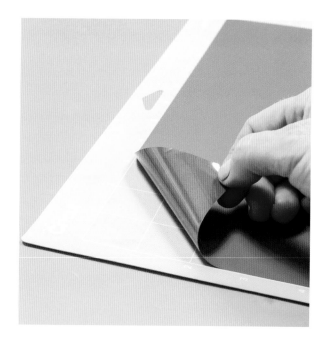

WEEDING HTV

In the last chapter, you learned all about weeding (page 63). How is weeding HTV different? The process is basically the same! You are removing all the excess that you don't want on your project. This is often the excess around the outside and the centers of letters.

I actually find that weeding HTV is easier than weeding vinyl. That is the reason I choose this product for some of my wood crafts. It is just easier to use! Plus, you don't have to worry about your scrap pieces sticking to everything as they do with adhesive vinyl. As always, the items you weed away from your design will be thrown away and scrapped. If you want to save pieces from your sheet, be sure to trim those away with scissors before weeding.

HTV SETTINGS

Once your cut is complete and you've weeded out the excess material, you will need to activate the adhesive on this product with heat. So, what temperature and time should you use for application? That depends on the brand and type of HTV that you are using. I always recommend going to the manufacturer's website or the website where you purchased the product and looking at their instructions. For Cricut Iron-On, the Cricut Heat Guide on the Cricut website is a great resource. Input your material and blank types; the guide will then give you a list of instructions to follow for application.

I have seen times anywhere from 4 to 30 seconds and temperatures from 285 to 325°F (140 to 162°C). There are also products that you press from the front as well as the back. You want to follow all instructions, as you can overheat HTV. Find the instructions before beginning your project so you are prepared once you start pressing.

Often with the time and temperature requirements, you will see a pressure listed. Usually, it is listed as "light", "medium" or "heavy." What exactly does this mean? With an iron or handheld press, you will just have to go by feel. Light pressure is generally pushing down slightly. Medium pressure would be holding down with both hands. With heavy pressure, I always try to put as much of my weight on the project as I can. Heavy pressure is easier and more consistent with a traditional heat press. If you are finding that you are failing with projects that have this requirement, that is probably the root cause.

PEELING BACK THE CARRIER SHEET

Once you have pressed the HTV, you are probably excited to see your new creation. STOP! Sometimes you need to let the project cool so the adhesive can adhere to your base before peeling back that top sheet. It is hard to be patient, but it will be so worth it in the end. Again, you will want to check with the manufacturer to see what type of peel they recommend. Terms you may see include:

- Hot peel: Congrats, you can peel this right off of the press and don't have to wait!

- Warm peel: You will need to let it cool a bit before peeling. I would say 60 seconds or so.

- Cool or cold peel: The project needs to be at room temperature before you peel the carrier sheet back. This is where your patience comes in!

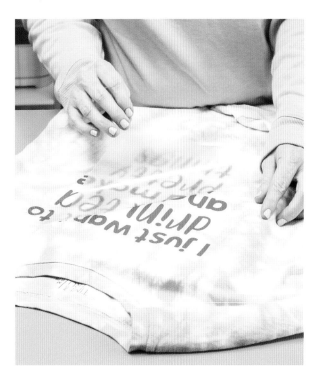

HTV TROUBLESHOOTING

The application of HTV is not hard, but it may take some practice. Here are some common mistakes and issues and how to fix them:

- The brand of HTV, the stickiness of your mat and the condition of your blade can all play into whether or not your project will cut correctly. Try cleaning your mat or pressing your material down well with the brayer. Clean your blade and make sure there is nothing stuck to it. Finally, you may consider switching brands if you continually have issues with a certain one.

- Double-check the instructions and make sure you are following each step.

- Replace any of the carrier sheet you have lifted up and press for a second time. Sometimes a second press is all that is needed to get the HTV to stick.

- Be sure to pre-press to remove moisture in the fabric that can prevent the HTV from sticking.

- If there are seams at the collar or sleeves of your shirt, most likely the press is sitting up off of the surface and not making contact. Try adding a mat inside of your shirt to raise it up a bit for pressing.

- Check your heat source to make sure it is working correctly, coming to the right temperature and has consistent heat across the surface.

- With larger designs, remember that each area of the design will need to be pressed for the full time. I like to slightly overlap the press area, which means that the middle portion will get pressed more than once.

- For textured or uneven surfaces, I like to rub the surface with a scraper while it is hot. That will usually force it down into those small textured areas.

- Try pressing again but this time using more pressure than is called for. Sometimes you need a bit of extra pressure to get the material down onto the surface.

- You may have to wash your fabric surface before application. Stores or manufacturers sometimes add a coating to their products that prevent HTV from sticking.

- As a last resort, try increasing the time or temperature recommendations. Do this with caution as you can overheat the product and ruin your project!

BEYOND THE BASICS

I know that you will be hooked on HTV projects once you get the hang of it. Here are a few advanced options to expand your crafting!

- **Layering:** While layering on top of glitter, foil or flock doesn't work well, other HTV types can be layered several times. Start with the Layered HTV Tote Bag (page 97) to get the hang of the basics.

- **Application hacks:** From placing your design to putting your layers together, there are several hacks you can try to make your project perfect! See one idea for locating HTV correctly on a shirt in the Crafty HTV Shirt (page 93).

- **Print your own designs at home:** While printable HTV is not perfect, it is a great option if you have an inkjet printer at home. See the Zipper Pouch (page 177) for a project using this product.

- **Think outside of shirts:** There are so many more surfaces to add HTV to! One example is the Wood Door Hanger (page 107).

Are you ready to learn how to use HTV to make something amazing? The projects in this chapter will give you the foundation to start creating gorgeous designs for yourself as well as family and friends.

CRAFTY HTV SHIRT

Level: Beginner

Machine requirements: Any Cricut machine

Skills: Using HTV, light box, templates, locating HTV

Challenge: After you complete the Layered HTV Tote Bag (page 97), come back and make a shirt with HTV layers.

Supplies Needed

Shirt

Shirt ruler (optional)

HTV (in the colors of your choice)

Fine point blade

Light grip (blue) Cricut mat

Weeding tools

Light box (optional)

Iron, EasyPress or other heat press

EasyPress mat or towel

A shirt is the number one thing that people who purchase a Cricut want to make. In this project, I'm making an extra special shirt and giving it a crafty theme! Remember you can mix and match the design if you would like to create something all your own.

I. Upload the shirt SVG found at cricuthandbook.com to Cricut Design Space using the skills you have learned on page 55. Alternatively, you can make your own design and just follow along with the instructions below. I am going to use two different colors of HTV for my design so I changed the colors in Cricut Design Space.

Note: When you import an SVG, you may have to click "ungroup" in the right toolbar to alter each layer. Make sure to attach the like colors together.

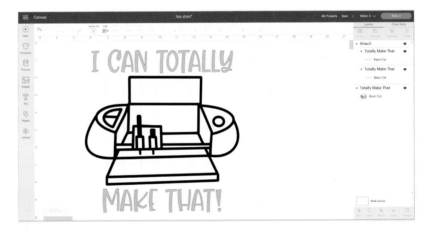

1

(continued)

2

3

4

2. Be sure to size your design to fit your shirt. There are a few different ways to do this. You can measure your shirt with a ruler and size to fit. Or you can use the template feature in Cricut Design Space. Click "templates" on the left toolbar.

Note: *Templates are not available on the mobile app.*

3. Pick the item that is closest to what you will be using. This will put a template onto your canvas. Click the template name in the lower right-hand corner to open up the options. Change these options to match the blank you are using.

Note: *This template will not cut with your design.*

4. Then arrange and resize your design until it looks good on the shirt. You can double-check these measurements with a ruler on your actual shirt before cutting. Click "make it." On the next screen, be sure to click "mirror" on each mat to mirror your design.

5. Then click "continue" and use the basic cutting instructions on page 26. Design Space will always remind you to mirror when you choose an Iron-On material type. Be sure to put the HTV on the mat shiny side down as shown on page 88.

5

6. I trimmed away the excess around my design to use for a future project, and now it is time to weed away the outside and the centers of any letters. If you have trouble seeing the cut lines, a light box is a great investment. You will find this extremely useful for glitter vinyl and HTV as the cut lines can be hard to see. Remember, you will be turning this over to iron it on, so at this point it should appear backwards.

7. Once you are ready to press, be sure to look up the instructions for the brand of HTV you are using for the best results. Then preheat your press or iron. In this case, I am putting an EasyPress mat inside of my shirt to press from the front. This will ensure that the seams do not interfere with pressing.

Note: When pressing two different types of HTV, use the time and temperature that is the greatest.

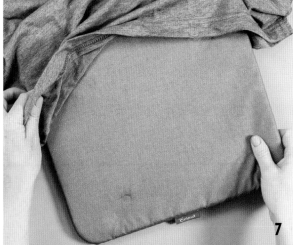

8. First, press the shirt for 10 to 15 seconds to remove any moisture and wrinkles from the surface. In this case, my shirt is cotton so it is fine coming in contact with the heat press surface. If you are using a delicate material for your blank, use a Teflon sheet or even a pressing cloth to keep the surface of the press from touching the fabric.

When pressing more than one color, if the colors do not overlap, you can press them at one time. To do this, trim the carrier sheets so they do not overlap. Here I have trimmed the sheet for the inside design so it does not touch the words at all. Then add your design to your shirt with the carrier sheet on top. A shirt ruler is a great way to make sure your design is straight and in the right location.

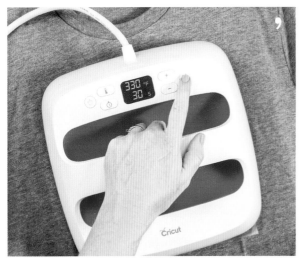

9. The carrier sheet on the HTV is sticky and this will help hold it in place. Add your EasyPress or iron to the top or put your entire shirt in your heat press. The carrier sheet is also heat resistant so it can touch your heating source.

10. Then just follow all instructions for your HTV for time, temperature and pressure as well as any special instructions, like pressing from the back. Once you have pressed your shirt, peel back the carrier sheet. Check the peel temperature as discussed on page 90. As you peel back the carrier sheet, be sure to watch and make sure your HTV is staying on your surface. If it is not, try the troubleshooting tips on pages 90 and 91.

You may have to peel the carrier sheet for the second color separately, as they may not peel off all at one time. For your first shirt, feel free to start with just a single-color design. I wanted to add another color to illustrate the process. This pressing method avoids a ton of location errors as well as issues with the HTV or shirt shrinking when pressed. Once the carrier sheets are off, your shirt is ready to wear! There is nothing further needed for using HTV on fabric surfaces like shirts.

LAYERED HTV TOTE BAG

Level: Beginner

Machine requirements: Any Cricut machine

Skills: Layering HTV, offset, uploading fonts, contour, heat transfer mask

Challenge: Use the offset function and some fonts on your computer to create a few more designs for tote bags, shirts and so much more.

Supplies Needed

HTV (in the colors of your choice)

Fine point blade

Light grip (blue) Cricut mat

Weeding tools

Heat transfer mask (if using certain brands of patterned HTV)

Iron, EasyPress or other heat press

EasyPress mat or towel

Tote bag

Are you ready to layer some HTV? Layer different colors and even patterns to get a look that is unique and all your own. Just remember that products like glitter, foil, flock and certain other specialty HTV products should only be the top layer.

1. Let's start by uploading some fonts for use on this project. I am using a monogram font that has a left, right and center version to make circular monograms easy. First, find a font you like and download the file. This file may be a ZIP file that will need to be unzipped in order to use it. Please note that unzipping can be done for free and you do not need to pay for software to do this.

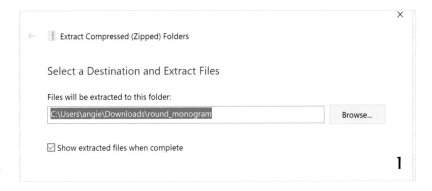

1

(continued)

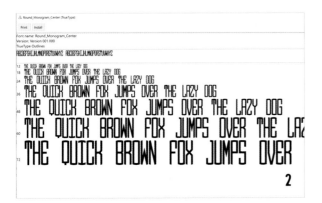

2

3

4

5

2. Once unzipped, you will see some font files and usually a licensing file. See page 31 for licensing information. The font files will often be in two types: OTF and TTF. For a Cricut, the best choice is OTF, but TTF fonts will also work. On a PC, double-click the font file and click "install." On a Mac, double-click the font file, which will open it in Font Book, and then click "install font."

3. Once the fonts are installed, they will automatically appear in the system fonts area in Cricut Design Space. If you have Design Space open, you will probably need to close and restart for them to appear. If you still do not see them, uncheck the "kerned fonts only" box, as that setting will hide some fonts.

4. Add each of the letters for your monogram to the canvas. Here I am using each of the three different monogram fonts (left, right and center). These can all be set to the same font size and moved together to make a monogram in minutes. Remember that monograms are first initial, last initial and then middle initial.

5. Now that you have your monogram, let's add some layers. First, pick all three monogram pieces and attach them together. Then click "offset" in the top toolbar. You will see a box pop up with options. Here I am doing a small external offset that is welded with rounded corners. Feel free to play with the options in this box to get a feel for what each controls.

Note: *Currently offset is not available on the mobile app.*

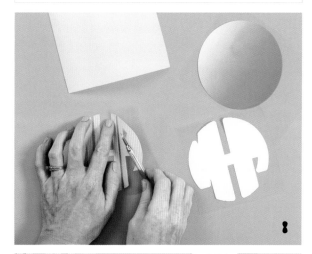

6. Click "apply" and you will have added an offset to your canvas. Highlight the offset and click "contour" in the bottom right toolbar. You can now pick any cuts that you want to hide. This is a great way to customize your project easily. Just click the center of the A and click the "X" in the top right-hand corner, for example.

7. Finally, I used the shape tool to make a circle behind the monogram for a third layer. This one is now ready to cut!

8. Cut each layer of HTV on your Cricut machine using the basic cutting instructions on page 26. Remember to mirror each of your designs before cutting. There is one exception to this rule, however. The printed HTV that I am using for the bottom layer does not have a mask on top so it does NOT need to be mirrored when cutting. Always look at the instructions for patterned or printed HTV before cutting. Weed each layer using weeding tools to remove all excess from around the outside edge as well as the centers of any letters.

9. For the bottom layer, I need to apply the heat transfer mask to get the cut piece onto my tote bag. Remember that this is not regular transfer tape. You will need a special mask that is heat resistant, and you can read more about these options on page 86. You do, however, apply it just like transfer tape. So apply it to the top of your HTV and burnish it down well. Then remove the backing from the HTV, leaving it on the transfer mask.

10.

10. I am adding the monogram to the center of this tote. One hack for finding the center of any blank is to fold it when preheating. Fold in half in both directions and press for just a few seconds. This will give you a center mark on your tote bag.

11. Then just add your first layer to the center of the bag and press according to the directions for that type of HTV. When layering, however, you want to press the bottom layers for as little time as possible. Usually, you can press at the right temperature for about half the time and the HTV will stick enough so you can remove the carrier sheet. This also helps with any shrinking as you press the multiple layers.

11

12. Add the second layer on top of the first and press again. Make sure that your entire bottom layer is covered when pressing any layers on top of it. You can use a Teflon sheet to cover it or just save the mask from the bottom layer and apply it on top before pressing.

13. When adding your top layer, press for the entire time at the right temperature. This will ensure that your top layer as well as any layers underneath are adhered well. Don't forget to cover the entire thing with your carrier sheet or a Teflon sheet. Once you peel back the carrier sheet from your top layer, your tote bag is complete.

12

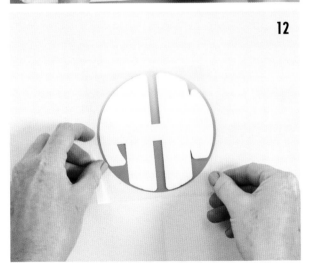

13

REVERSE CANVAS

Level: Intermediate

Machine requirements: Any Cricut machine

Skills: Large HTV projects, using Smart Iron-On

Challenge: Upload some additional fonts to create your own design instead of or in addition to the examples here.

Supplies Needed

Canvas (in any size)

Screwdriver

Pliers

Spray paint

Smart Iron-On or regular HTV (in the colors of your choice)

Fine point blade

Light grip (blue) Cricut mat (if you are not using Smart Iron-On)

Scissors

Weeding tools

Iron, EasyPress or other heat press

EasyPress mat or towel

Staple gun or hot glue gun

A reverse canvas can be a gorgeous addition to your home's décor and this one is extra-large to make a big impact. In this project, I am illustrating how to use Smart Iron-On with the Maker 3 or Explore 3. If you have another machine, just slice the designs into smaller pieces to fit on the mat, then use the same methods for pressing.

I. Disassemble your canvas by flipping it over to the back and removing the staples with a screwdriver and some pliers. Alternatively, you can use a craft knife to cut the canvas away.

1

(continued)

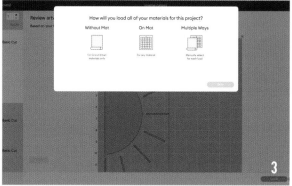

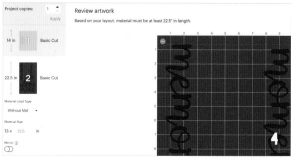

2. Once the canvas is removed, take the frame out and flip it over. It is always a surprise when you open up a canvas—you can get a variety of looks which I think is part of the fun of this project. You can stain or paint the frame if you'd like. I prefer to paint the frame as there will probably be exposed staples and even writing on your frame once you remove it from the canvas. If you like a more rustic look, stain may be a better option for you.

3. Use the skills you've already learned to upload one or both of the SVG files from cricuthandbook.com for this project (see page 55). Resize them to fit the frame you just removed. Also be sure to attach any like colors together so they cut correctly. Then click "make it." This time I am picking "without a mat" as I am using Smart Iron-On. You can use any HTV that you would like by just adding it to a mat and making sure your pieces are sized to fit.

4. Design Space will tell you how much of each material you will need. Be sure you have this much left on any rolls you are using, otherwise the machine will not cut.

5. To cut Smart Materials, just load them into your machine without a mat. You can use the roll holder (sold separately) if you would like but it is not required. Smart Iron-On is still cut with the shiny side down, and the cuts should be mirrored. The machine will measure the material, then start cutting.

6. Cut each of your colors with your Cricut machine. Then trim away any excess HTV with scissors and weed each of your designs. Remove everything around the outside as well as the centers of any letters.

7. You can add the HTV to either side of the canvas. I tend to pick the white side for a cleaner look and the cream side for a more rustic project. You will want to put the design approximately in the center, but you can adjust some once you add the frame later. Pre-heating does not apply to materials like this as a general rule. This is a great place to use a Teflon sheet to cover your project before pressing as you will not know the material of the canvas.

8. For these large designs, press multiple times to cover the entire area. You can make them even with a small press or iron. Just be sure you overlap each press so that no areas go without the proper heat being applied. Once you have pressed over your entire design, remove the carrier sheet. If you have issues getting your HTV to stick, see the troubleshooting tips on page 90. Remember that this is going to be one of those materials that may need some experimentation, as you don't know exactly what the canvas is made of.

9. I applied one color to my canvas, removed the carrier sheet, then layered over a second color. Be sure to use something to cover the first layer when pressing, like a Teflon sheet or an old carrier sheet.

10. Once again, the HTV is too large for my Easy-Press, but I pressed several times, overlapping each press slightly. Remove the carrier sheet from this second layer and it is time to add the frame. Locate the frame so that your design is in the center. Then you can either use a staple gun or a hot glue gun to secure it into place. Remember to pull the canvas tight, however, as you don't want any wrinkles.

11. Trim away any excess canvas material with a craft knife. Then flip over your canvas and hang it on your wall. In a few minutes, you have a gorgeous piece of art for your home! You can repeat with the other SVG included for this project or make a design all your own.

Level: Advanced

Machine requirements: Any Cricut machine

Skills: Adding HTV to wood, finding free images, curving text, changing material size

Challenge: Use the SVG files from the previous project to make some art on wood as well. Experiment with adding HTV to wood and see if you like it better than adhesive vinyl.

Supplies Needed

Wood round

Paint or stain

HTV (in the color of your choice) (one with a lower time and temperature for application works best here)

Fine point blade

Light grip (blue) Cricut mat

Crepe paper (you can substitute regular paper or felt)

Pink fabric mat (only if you are using crepe paper)

Brayer

Rotary blade (only if you are using crepe paper)

Tweezers

Iron, EasyPress or other heat press (the smaller the better for wood)

Weeding tools

Scraper

Sealer (optional)

Paintbrush (only for applying sealer)

Paper glue

Hot glue and glue gun

WOOD DOOR HANGER

I personally love changing up my door décor for every season, so this project is one of my favorites. Here I am using crepe paper with my Cricut Maker; however, you can use regular paper or even felt instead. Either way, it will look gorgeous on your door any time of the year!

I. Paint or stain your wood round at least 24 hours before you are going to make your project. This will ensure that the paint is cured and all moisture is removed for HTV application. To make your design, click "images" on the left toolbar in Design Space and search for "leaf" at the top. Then use the filters on the left to find only free images. Pick one of these leaf shapes for your project by clicking it, then clicking "add to canvas." You can make as many copies of this and colors as you would like.

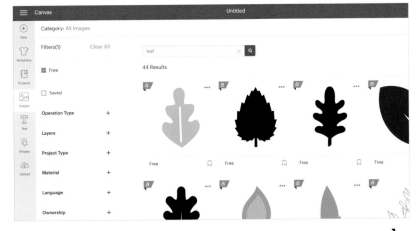

1

(continued)

2

2. Then add text for your door hanger. I am using two lines of text for my version. I also added a circle the size of my wood round. Pick the second line of text and click "curve" in the top toolbar. Play with this slider until you get the text as curved as you would like it to be.

   Note: *Curved text is not on the mobile version of the app.*

3

3. Be sure your text is in the location that you would like it to be on your final project, then delete the circle from your canvas. Pick both lines of text and click "attach." I also added several of the flowers used on page 80 to my canvas. I kept these as large as I could cut them given the size of my crepe paper. Remember, you can use regular cardstock if you don't have a Maker machine. The Maker series is the only one that can cut crepe paper.

   Note: *Make the flower as large as you possibly can, as the tight turns can cause digging into the mat. The mat can still be used, but this should be minimized if at all possible.*

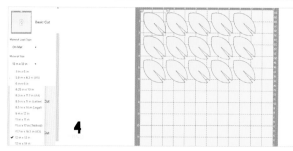

4

4. Click "make it." Be sure to mirror your text on just the mat that has the HTV design. Also, if your crepe paper is an odd size, be sure to pull down the material size box and change it to reflect something that is close to the right size. This will automatically rearrange your leaves to fit so that you are cutting just on the paper and not on the mat.

5

5. Click "continue" and be sure to pick crepe paper as your setting for those mats if you are using it. Otherwise, pick the setting for the material that you are cutting. To cut crepe paper, you will need to add it to the fabric grip mat. This material is very delicate and any other mat will tear it. Be sure to use a brayer to push it down onto the mat. If you are using another paper, use the skills you have already learned in this book to cut your pieces.

Welcome

PLEASE LEAVE BY 9

6. Cut the crepe paper in your Maker or Maker 3 using the rotary blade. This is the only blade that can be used, as the others will tear your material. You will also need to move the star wheels all the way to the right, as they can tear the paper as well. To remove the crepe paper from the mat, I find that lifting it with a pair of tweezers from the edge then pulling works well.

7. Preheat your iron or EasyPress. Then cut the HTV for this project. Be sure to mirror your cut and put your material face down on the mat. Then weed away all of the excess from your material including everything around the outside, as well as the centers of any letters.

8. Apply your HTV to the door hanger first. Locate your design then cover it with a Teflon sheet. The Teflon will keep you from applying heat directly to the wood. Heat each area of your design for the time indicated by the HTV. Remember that this will be a bit of an experiment, but start with that time.

9. While the HTV is hot, rub over it with a scraper, pushing down slightly. This will push the HTV into the imperfections of the wood and give you better adhesion.

10. The HTV will take longer to cool down as the wood will hold the heat longer than other materials. Be sure to follow the instructions on the HTV you are using for peel temperature; however, you may find that allowing it to cool a bit more than indicated helps it stick to the wood. Attempt to peel back the carrier sheet.

11. If the HTV sticks to the wood, remove the carrier sheet. If it does not, replace the carrier sheet and repeat the heating process. Burnish more with the scraper, pushing down a bit more. Then try a different peel temperature than before, possibly allowing it to cool down before attempting to remove. All of these factors will depend on the HTV brand that you are using for your project.

12. Once the carrier sheet is removed, you can add the Teflon sheet over the top and secure any loose areas. Then allow the wood round to cool completely. At this point, if you are putting your project outdoors, seal the wood with a few coats of a Polycrylic or your favorite sealer. To assemble the leaves, add paper glue along the cut line down the center then fold it over onto itself. Set aside and allow to dry.

13. You can follow the instructions on page 80 to make the flowers. This time, however, you will not be able to let the flower expand out at the end to the size you want. If you are using crepe paper, it will need to be tightly wrapped, as the material will not expand. Add hot glue to the circle after rolling and then flip any excess up like another petal. Then you can fold some of the outer petals toward the outside to make the flower look more realistic. Protect crepe paper flowers from moisture by using them indoors or in a covered area.

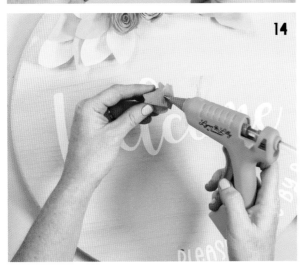

14. Use a hot glue gun to attach the flowers and leaves to your door hanger. Add a hanger to the back of the wood round then put on your door or anywhere else in your home!

INFUSIBLE INK

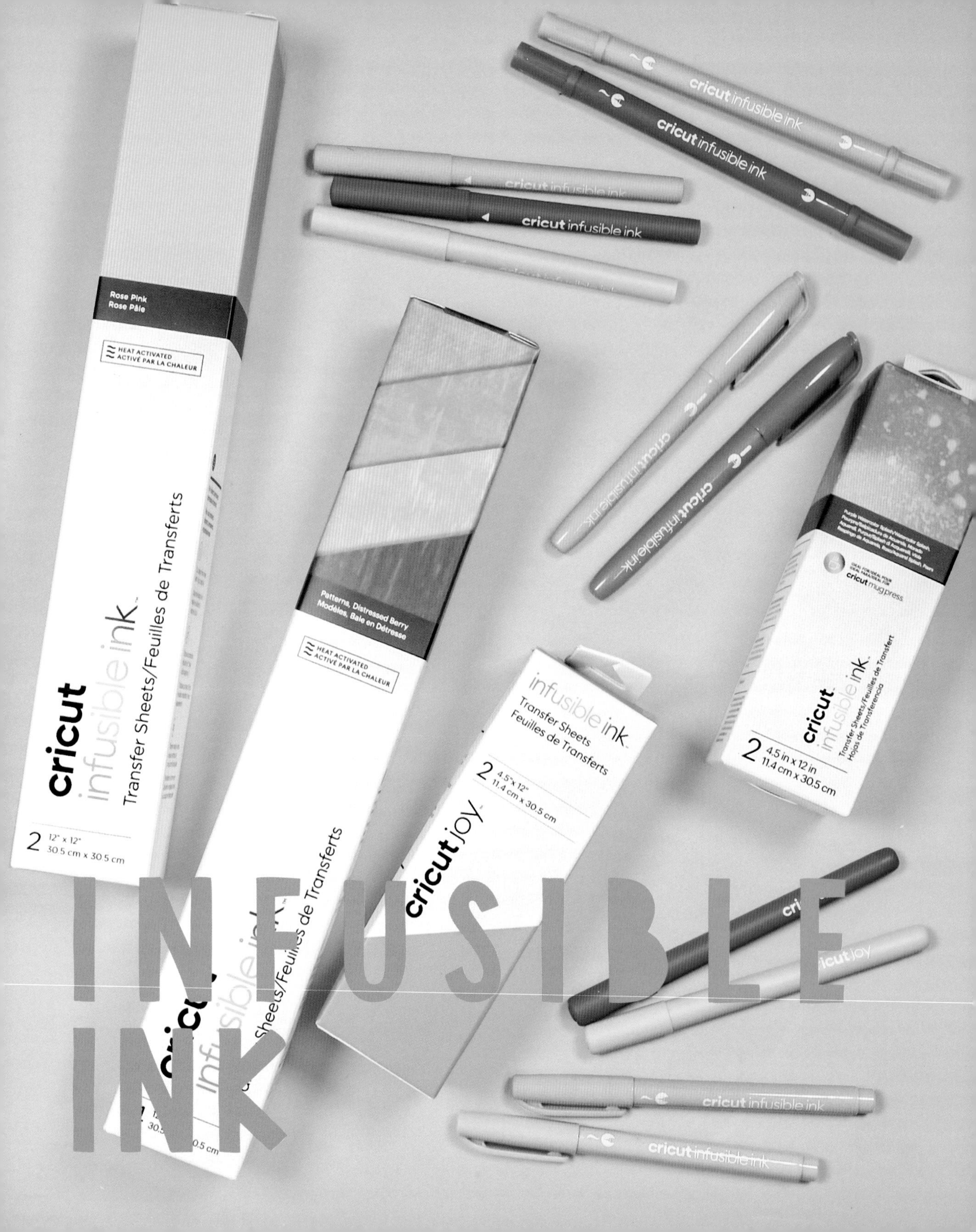

Ready to expand into another medium? Infusible Ink may be unlike any product you have ever seen! It does, however, have a learning curve. Follow this chapter from start to finish to work your way from beginner to advanced with this material.

INFUSIBLE INK BASICS

WHAT IS INFUSIBLE INK?

Infusible Ink is the Cricut version of sublimation. I look at it as sublimation for those that do not have a sublimation printer. But what is sublimation? Sublimation is a special ink that when heated reacts with the polyester on any surface to create a permanent bond. This means that Infusible Ink will turn into a gas and actually bond with the polyester fibers on your surface. This fusing of the materials means this is an extremely permanent form of crafting!

Also, because Infusible Ink fuses with your surface, it isn't raised on the surface like vinyl or HTV. In fact, you can't feel it at all when you run your hand across the surface. It is also permanent once the project is complete with no other steps required. If you are looking for long-lasting and dishwasher-safe projects, this is the chapter for you!

INFUSIBLE INK BRANDS AND TYPES

You have a few choices when it comes to Infusible Ink and your craft projects:

- Infusible Ink Sheets: These sheets are made to be cut with your Cricut machine, then applied to your surface. They are used differently than HTV, so you will want to follow all of the steps. When purchasing these sheets, be sure to go by the color that is on the outside of the box, as the sheets themselves will be muted until after pressing. Sizes are 12 x 12 inch (30.5 x 30.5 cm) large sheets and 4.5 x 12 inch (11.4 x 30.5 cm) small sheets. You can use any of these on any of the machines or for any project as long as your design will fit. For example, you may find some boxes marked for Cricut Joy or Mug Press specifically. These only indicate sheet sizes and do not exclude other machines or project types.

- Infusible Ink Pens and Markers: There are a wide variety of Infusible Ink pens and markers that you can use with your Cricut. Some of these go in your machine and others can be used to color by hand or draw your own creations. Remember that the colors will be muted when drawing with these and intensify when you apply heat.

Infusible Ink itself is a patented term from Cricut and I will be using it in this book to refer to the broad range of products on the market. You can also find sublimation markers as well as other brands of pre-printed sublimation sheets. Be sure to follow all directions on any of the products that you choose to use.

You may notice that the sheets come in a box with a black bag inside. It is important to keep this product dry and out of direct light. Be sure it is not stored in an overly humid area, as moisture is an enemy to Infusible Ink. You will also want to make sure your hands are clean and dry when handling the sheets during crafting.

INFUSIBLE INK TOOLS

You may have used some of these tools with the projects in a previous chapter, but it is worth mentioning them once again. You can see more details about beginner tools on page 20.

- Tweezers
- Brayer
- Lint roller
- Butcher paper and/or copy paper
- Heat resistant tape (this MUST BE heat resistant)
- Laser copy paper (needs to say it is good for laser printers on the back of the package)

For Infusible ink, you will also need a heat source for application. I recommend something that goes up to 400°F (204° C). Due to inconsistent heat, I would not recommend a home iron for Infusible Ink. There are a few options you can find under Heat Sources and Accessories (page 21) along with options for mats to put under your project.

WHAT CAN YOU PUT INFUSIBLE INK ON

The number one mistake I see with Infusible Ink is trying to add it to the wrong type of surface. You MUST have something with some polyester content for the chemical reaction to happen. Cricut does make its own line of blanks but there are so many more options on the market.

- **Polyester fabric:** I recommend at least 75 percent polyester content in your fabric for the best results. Less than 65 percent polyester content and you will probably be unhappy with the look of your final project. There are so many new things on the market made from polyester—you will be amazed when you start looking! I have even found shirts that feel just like cotton that can be used for sublimation.

- **Sublimation blanks:** Everything from mugs to tumblers to coasters and more come with a sublimation coating on them. While mugs from Dollar Tree® will not work with this product, you can find a wide variety of mugs with a poly coating on the market that will work.

- **Sublimatable HTV:** Infusible Ink can be applied to the top of some types of HTV, like glitter and flocked. There are also some special types of HTV that are on the market just for this purpose. Use this for adding Infusible Ink to cotton fabrics, dark colors and other things that would not traditionally work.

White is the most common sublimation blank color. This is because Infusible Ink is translucent after it is applied. You can use some light-colored blanks, but remember that the color of the blank will alter the color of your Infusible Ink.

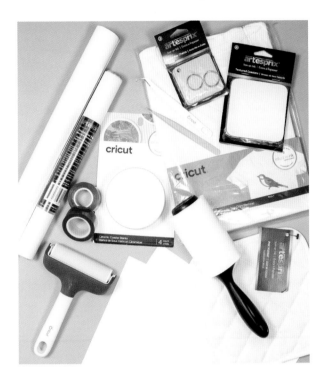

DESIGNS THAT WORK BEST

Infusible Ink sheets will work way better with simple designs. Thin lines and intricate details will not cut and weed well with this product. For those thinner details, try the pens and markers instead. I also recommend starting with designs that will fit under the heat source you have. You can work your way up to more complicated projects as you gain confidence.

HOW TO PUT INFUSIBLE INK SHEETS ON THE MAT

The standard grip mat is best for cutting this material. Infusible Ink sheets should be placed with the ink side up on the mat. The carrier sheet should be applied to the sticky part of your mat. You may find that these sheets curl quite a bit, so I recommend using your brayer to get them to lie flat.

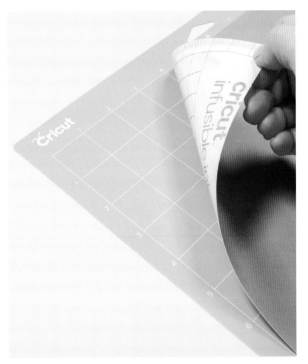

CUT SETTINGS FOR INFUSIBLE INK SHEETS

This product cuts with the fine point blade, and there is a cut setting for Infusible Ink sheets in Cricut Design Space. You want to cut through the ink portion of the sheet but not the carrier sheet. So, this will be a kiss cut very similar to HTV, and you want to mirror your design in the same manner.

Each color of Infusible Ink may cut differently, which makes this product a bit troublesome. You may have to choose "more" or "less" pressure after picking your material setting to get it to cut correctly. There are times when I have to cut my sheets with a second pass. You can always do this by pressing the "go" button on your machine another time before unloading the mat. I highly recommend a small test cut with this product, especially when using a new color or new blade.

WEEDING INFUSIBLE INK SHEET

This product weeds differently than HTV. Put down your weeding tools, as you will not need them for Infusible Ink! After you cut the sheets, remove them from the mat and then bend the sheets to crack your cut lines (you will actually hear a cracking sound). I like to crack the sheets in both directions. This is very important for easier weeding.

After cracking, start removing all of the pieces you don't want to be transferred to your design. The best method for doing this is with your (clean and dry) fingers. You can also use tweezers if you would like. Sharp weeding tools, however, can scratch the ink surface. Once scratched, you can get those bits of ink in places you don't want on your design.

When you are removing pieces, if the ink starts to separate and you see a white film, try removing from the opposite side or cracking the cut line some more by bending. A little of this white paper will be okay, but you don't want a lot of it on your final piece for pressing.

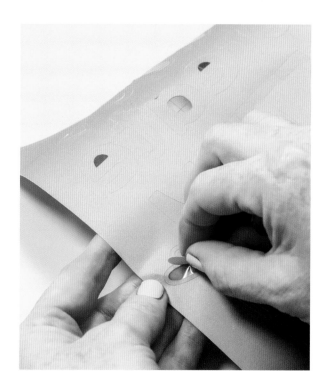

PREPPING YOUR BLANK

Now that you have purchased some blanks according to the specifications, you will want to prep them accordingly. There are a few important things to remember:

- Blanks must be clean and free from dirt or lint. I like to use a lint roller on all surfaces (even brand-new items) before applying Infusible Ink. You can also clean hard surfaces with rubbing alcohol, but remember to allow them to dry completely.

- Remove all moisture from any blank you are using. That may mean allowing it to dry completely or prepressing any fabrics with your heat press. Remember that moisture can wreak havoc on your final design.

- Infusible Ink is permanent after pressing, so you will want to make sure you get everything in the correct location the first time.

ADDING PROTECTIVE PAPER

You always want to protect your pressing pad, heat press and even the back of your shirt from any additional ink. Protective paper should be used on the bottom as well as the top of your blank. There are a few options to choose from:

- Butcher paper is common and comes inside the box of Infusible Ink sheets. If you want to purchase extra, get the white uncoated paper.

- Copy paper can be used on top as it is thin enough for moisture to escape.

- Sublimation protective paper is specifically made for this job and comes in rolls. I find that it works really well.

- White cardstock can be used under your design or inside of something like a shirt, but you do not want to use this product between the Infusible Ink and heat source, as it is too thick.

Now that you know what can be used, let's talk about what can't be used. You don't want to use parchment paper, wax paper, freezer paper or Teflon sheets. All of these have very different properties than butcher paper. You also don't want to use any paper that is colored, as heat can transfer that color to your surface.

PRESSING INFUSIBLE INK

Allow your base material to cool completely from the prepress before applying your design. Add your weeded design to your blank with the ink side down. You want to make sure it can't move at all, as any movement will ruin your project. You can use heat resistant tape to hold it in place. The carrier sheet of the Infusible Ink sheets is adhesive; however, you may also want to add a few pieces of tape to make sure nothing moves.

Note: *Some blanks are also placed upside down. On these, the Infusible Ink sheet will be on the bottom instead of the top when you are pressing. Make sure you read all instructions carefully before trying to add a design to your blank.*

I recommend the Cricut Heat Guide on the Cricut website for choosing the time and temperature for Infusible Ink. If you are using a blank that Cricut does not make, pick a blank that is the closest to what you are using. If you are using another brand of sublimation sheet or marker, be sure to see their instructions for use.

As with HTV, you need to make sure you follow any specific pressure requirements. For instance, on some Cricut blanks it says to push down, and on others it says to just set the heat press on top and let it sit. Be sure to read carefully to see how hard you need to press.

Once your items have been pressed, they will be extremely hot. Allowing your blank to cool is the safest course of action. Then you can just peel back the paper and the carrier sheet without issue. If you need to remove it warm, allow the item to cool some, then use heat-resistant gloves while peeling back. Once you peel back the Infusible Ink carrier sheet, you may see bits and pieces of the Infusible Ink sheet that remain on your project. You can lift those off with tweezers.

USING INFUSIBLE INK MARKERS

Infusible Ink markers are used in a similar way to the sheets, but there are a few things to keep in mind:

- Use your Cricut machine to draw with the pens and markers on copy paper. You want to make sure this paper is okay for use in laser printers so that it can withstand the heat from the pressing process.

- Always mirror Infusible Ink designs!

- Look for writing fonts and images that are a single line for best results when drawing in your Cricut machine.

- Once you draw with the pens, you can use more Infusible Ink markers to fill in your design or even freehand draw a design on a fresh piece of paper. If you freehand words, numbers or anything directional, you will need to mirror them.

- The paper may bleed more than the sheets, so you may want to add a couple of pieces of protective paper over your design to protect your press.

- You cannot just color directly on your surface with these markers. They are designed to be colored onto paper and transferred using heat.

INFUSIBLE INK TROUBLESHOOTING

Here are some common issues with Infusible Ink. This is a great place to start if you are having issues:

- Double-check the instructions on the Cricut Heat Guide. Are you following all of the steps exactly?

- Make sure you have a polyester or poly-coated blank. There are also poor-quality sublimation blanks on the market, and that can cause issues.

- Faded areas in your transfer can be caused by moisture. Be sure everything is clean and dry and that you prepress your fabric.

- Does your project look like it has spots? That is most likely lint or debris on your surface.

- A double print is called ghosting. Tape the sheets down well to prevent any movement and allow your project to cool before removing the ink. Prepress to ensure your blank is not shrinking when pressed. Be sure to allow your blank to cool after prepressing, as ink can start to transfer to a warm blank.

- For any fading, make sure your press is not on the seams of your blank or otherwise not making adequate contact. Make sure you are on a flat and even surface when pressing. Also try pressing your design only once and not moving your press.

The question now is how do you fix the project you just messed up? I will say it is fairly difficult to fix any issues. You can try pressing again or adding a black design over any mistakes. After all, if the blank is already scrap, you might as well try to save it!

BEYOND THE BASICS

Now that we have covered the basics of this material, let's look at some advanced techniques that you may try after a few projects.

- **Layering:** It is possible to use more than one color of Infusible Ink sheet, but the best way to do this is unlike any other layering you have done so far. See Silhouette Coasters (page 129) for an example.

- **Application hacks:** You can use the same application hacks that you learned for HTV for Infusible Ink.

- Use this chapter to get comfortable with this craft medium, then branch out to other surfaces for your next Infusible Ink project.

Now it is time to grab some Infusible Ink and start trying it out! Remember that simple designs will be the easiest with this material, so don't get too complicated too quickly.

INFUSIBLE INK SHIRTS

Level: Beginner

Machine requirements: Any Cricut machine

Skills: Basics of Infusible Ink sheets

Challenge: Start with these simple designs, then experiment with some other designs using the skills you have learned so far.

Supplies Needed

EasyPress or other heat press

Infusible Ink sheets (in the color of your choice)

Medium grip (green) Cricut mat

Brayer (optional)

Fine point blade

Scissors

Tweezers

Shirts that are marked at least 75% polyester or for sublimation

EasyPress mat

Lint roller

Butcher paper (or any other protective paper)

Heat resistant tape

Infusible Ink is the best for wearable crafts, as it will not fade and will last as long as the shirt lasts! So, grab those polyester shirts and start adding some designs to the front. I know you will love how they turn out! You might want to grab several shirts, as everyone who sees them will want you to make them one as well.

I. Preheat your EasyPress or heat press to the time and temperature in the Cricut Heat Guide indicated for shirts. Get the free SVG for these shirts at cricuthandbook.com and upload it to Cricut Design Space using the instructions on page 55. Ungroup the file, as they will all come in together. You can then delete any designs that you do not want to cut. Resize the remaining designs to work on your shirts.

Pro Tip: I like to use a flexible measuring tape meant for sewing to measure the shirt area and make sure I get the correct size.

(continued)

2. Add the Infusible Ink sheet to the mat with the ink side up. Remember that your hands should be clean and dry when handling these sheets. You can go over the sheet with a brayer to press it down. I find that these sheets tend to curl and wrinkle when laid flat.

3. Then click "make it" in Design Space and mirror your cuts for each mat. Pick the Infusible Ink sheet setting in Cricut Design Space. Remember that these sheets can be tricky to cut through. You can do a test cut at this point by just cutting a small square in the corner of your sheet. Cut your design from the Infusible Ink sheet, then remove the mat from the machine. Remove the sheet from your mat and trim away any excess with scissors to use for another project.

4. Then bend the Infusible Ink so that the cut lines crack. You will hear a cracking noise as you do this. You may even see some pieces start to lift. That is okay! Just keep bending and cracking in both directions.

5. Then start using your hands to remove any small pieces first. It is generally easier to begin with the small pieces and work your way up to the larger pieces. Infusible Ink weeds slowly. Take your time and pull up each piece, making sure to remove all of the ink from any areas that you don't want transferred to your surface. You can use tweezers if you need to, but make sure not to scratch the surface of the ink.

6. Once all of the excess is removed, it is time to add your design to a shirt. Remember that shirts for this project should be at least 75 percent polyester and a light color for the best results. Add butcher paper or even cardstock to the inside of your shirt to protect the back. Lay the shirt on an EasyPress mat or folded-up towel. Lint roll the front of the shirt well to remove any and all debris from the surface.

7. Then prepress the shirt for 10 to 15 seconds to remove any moisture and wrinkles. Remember to put butcher paper down over the top of your shirt to protect the fabric. Remove the Easy-Press as well as the butcher paper and wait 15 to 30 seconds. Then add your Infusible Ink design with the ink side down on the front of the shirt. You can use some of the tricks from the HTV chapter for locating your design. The backing sheet of the Infusible Ink is slightly sticky. If it seems to be stuck to the shirt, you can leave it as is; however, if it feels like it could move, I suggest adding a couple pieces of heat resistant tape.

8. Add butcher paper over your design, then press your shirt at the correct temperature for the entire time indicated in the Cricut Heat Guide. Be sure not to move the EasyPress at all once you set it down on top of your shirt. You can press down, but you don't want to move from side to side.

9. Once the time is up, lift the press straight up so you move the Infusible Ink as little as possible. You have two options at this point. You can allow it to cool completely before touching anything, or you can allow it to cool for about 3 minutes, then peel back your design. Both methods should give you great results, but the ink may still be hot after 3 minutes.

10. After you peel back the carrier sheet and ink, use tweezers to remove any stray bits of the ink sheet that may still be on your shirt. Then your project is complete! This shirt is done and machine washable as soon as it is cool. Be sure to check the Cricut Heat Guide for care instructions for your new shirts.

INFUSIBLE INK MUG AND COASTER

Level: Beginner

Machine requirements: Any Cricut machine

Skills: Working with Infusible Ink and sublimation pens

Challenge: Experiment with writing fonts and make another design to work with this same project in Cricut Design Space.

Supplies Needed

Sublimation mug (diameter must fit the mug press)

Measuring tape

EasyPress or other heat press (for the coasters)

Cricut Mug Press (for the mug)

Infusible Ink and/or sublimation pens/markers (in the colors of your choice)

Copy paper (make sure it says it can be used in a laser printer on the back of the package)

Light grip (blue) Cricut mat

Scissors

Lint roller

Heat resistant tape

Butcher paper (or any other protective paper)

EasyPress Mat

Sublimation coasters

Let's break out those Infusible Ink or sublimation pens and make a couple of projects. I am actually adding two projects to this section, as one will use the Cricut Mug Press. If you don't have the Mug Press, give the coaster project a try instead. You can always make the matching set shown here if you have the supplies and equipment.

I. Upload the SVG file for this project to Cricut Design Space (for more on uploading files, see page 55). Once loaded, be sure that it measures correctly for your mug. Measure the mug using a sewing tape measure. Be sure that the design is kept 0.5 inch (12.7 mm) from the handle on both sides.

Note: I have made two versions of this design for the small and large Cricut mugs. If you have their brand of mugs, they should come in at the correct size.

(continued)

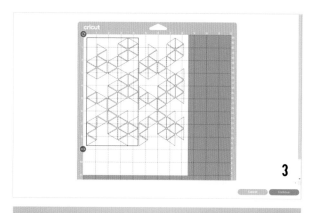

3

4

5

2. If using this file to make a coaster instead, you can use the shapes panel to draw a square in the same size as your coaster. Then lay the design over and use the "slice" function (page 38) to make the design the right size. Be sure to delete everything except for the draw lines for the coaster.

3. Before continuing, you will want to make sure that all of the lines are draw lines and not cut lines. Then click "make it" and be sure to mirror your design. Remember that even drawings with the pens will need to be mirrored as they will be placed face down on your surface. You will also want to change your material size to reflect the paper you are using so your design will fit on your page.

Note: Be sure to preheat your EasyPress, heat press or mug press to the right time and temperature according to the Cricut Heat Guide. The mug press just needs to be turned on, as it does not have a time or temperature setting.

4. Add your pen into your machine. Remember these need to be Infusible Ink pens and not the regular Cricut pens. Pick copy paper as your material and allow your machine to draw the design.

5. Once complete, remove the mat. Then remove your copy paper from the mat by turning it over and peeling the mat back. Now you have a super simple design for your project, but I wanted to make it extra special! I used some sublimation markers to color in some of my design. You can use these or Infusible Ink markers to color and draw on the paper. Remember that the colors change drastically once pressed.

Note: You may want to add some copy paper under your project, as the markers can bleed through your paper.

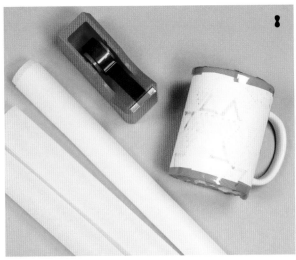

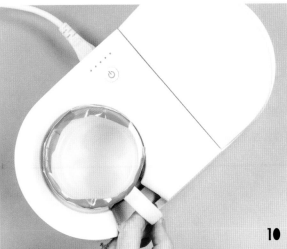

6. Your design is ready to press as soon as you are done adding color or drawings to the paper. Trim the paper with scissors. I like to trim right at the bottom of the design to help get it straight on the mug.

7. To make the mug, clean the surface well with a lint roller, then apply the design ink side down to the surface. Remember that the mug press will not press 0.5 inch (12.7 mm) from the mug handle on both sides. If you set your mug on a table and make sure the bottom of the design is touching the table, the design should be straight on the surface.

8. Once you have your design located, tape it down really well on your mug. It is important that this design does not move. I like to tape all the way around the bottom and several places on the top.

9. Then you need to cover the entire thing with several layers of butcher paper. I like to use four sheets, as the markers bleed more than the sheets. Add the butcher paper on top of your design and tape a few places so it doesn't move.

10. Add your mug to the mug press and press down the handle. Be sure the handle of the mug ends up in the center of the opening and that your entire design is covered by the heated portion of the press. The lights on the mug press will illuminate and start moving all the way across. This indicates the amount of time that is left.

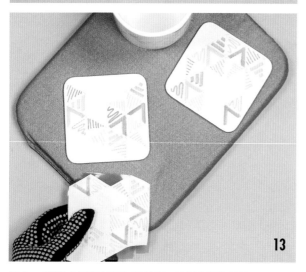

11. Once the mug press chimes, you can lift the handle and remove the mug. The handle will be cool to the touch. Set the mug on a heat-resistant mat and allow it to cool completely. Once cool, peel back the paper to reveal your gorgeous design! Again, this is permanent once pressed, plus it is dishwasher and microwave safe. There is nothing else you have to do with these mugs.

12. To make the coaster, clean the surface well with a lint roller, then apply the design with the ink against the white sublimation surface. Some coasters will come with a plastic protective film over the top, and you want to be sure to remove that before pressing. Tape the design down well with the heat resistant tape. I like to leave my paper a little large on the sides and tape to the excess.

13. Then add butcher paper to the top as well as the bottom of your coaster to catch any excess ink. Press with the EasyPress or a heat press at the recommended temperature for the correct time. Remove the press and let it cool for 3 minutes before removing the design. Alternately, you can allow it to cool completely, as the coaster will be hot for some time.

As with other Infusible Ink projects, this one is done once you remove the paper. The design is permanent and ready to be used!

SILHOUETTE COASTERS

Level: Intermediate

Machine requirements: Any Cricut machine

Skills: Layering Infusible Ink, background removal tool

Challenge: Now that you know how to layer Infusible Ink, try these same tricks to make another shirt with a more complicated design.

Supplies Needed

Infusible Ink sheets (in the colors of your choice)

Infusible Ink pens (in the colors of your choice)

Fine point blade

Medium grip (green) Cricut mat

EasyPress or other heat press

Scissors

Tweezers (optional)

Sublimation coasters

Lint roller

Heat resistant tape

EasyPress Mat

White cardstock

Butcher paper (or any other protective paper)

While layering Infusible Ink can be tricky, it also makes some of the most gorgeous designs ever! Here we are using a combination of the pens and sheets to make some amazing coasters that would make a great gift idea for just about anyone on your list. These ceramic coasters look really professional once completed, and they are so easy to customize!

1. Start by drawing circles the same size as the coasters that you will be sublimating. Then import pictures you want to use for the silhouettes using "upload" on the left toolbar. Click "upload" and find your image on your device. I usually click "complex" on the first screen for most images.

(continued)

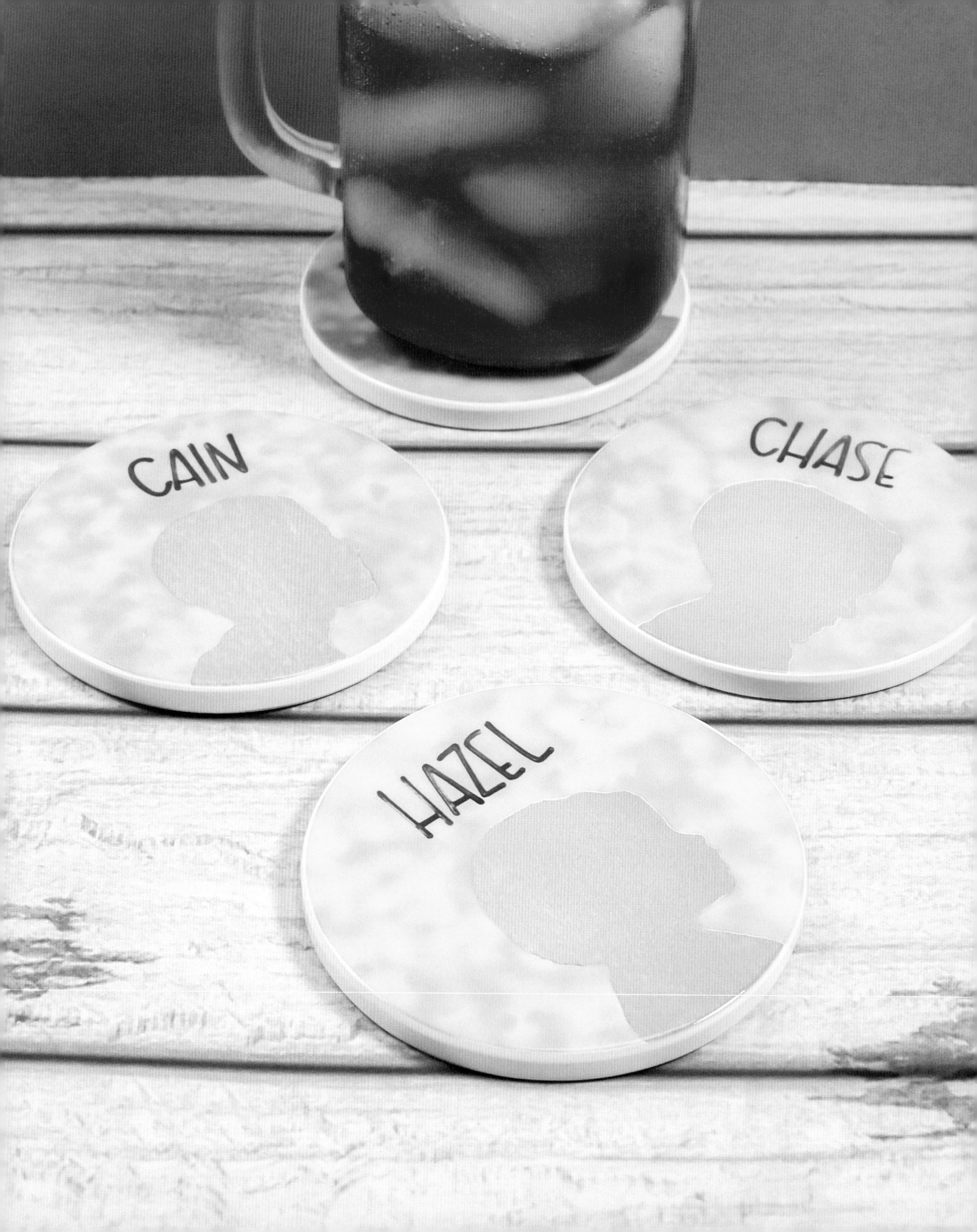
CAIN
CHASE
HAZEL

2. As you import each image, you will want to remove the background on this screen. You have two different options for doing this in Design Space, or you can use another website (like remove.bg) before importing. For option 1, use the automatic background removal tool. Just click "remove background" and Cricut does the work for you. This feature is only available to Access subscribers, but I have another option below that anyone can use. If the automatic background remover doesn't get your project correct, you can use the manual tools to remove any excess or add portions of your image back.

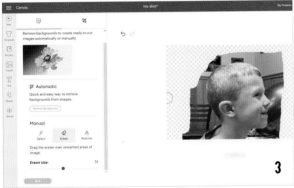

3. Option 2 is to manually remove the background in Cricut Design Space. To do this, I first like to crop the image to remove any excess around the outside. Then use the tools to start erasing the background from around the image. You can make the tool smaller or larger to get into the details around your image. Zoom in as needed to see the image.

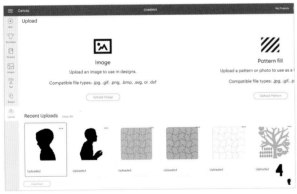

4. Once you are happy with your silhouette, click "continue" and then upload your project as a cut file. You will not need to print this, as we only need the outline. Pick the image on the next screen and click "add to canvas."

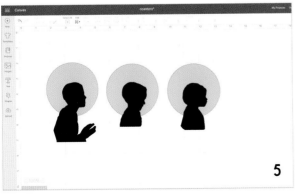

5. Continue with this same method for as many silhouettes as you would like for your coaster set. Resize each of your images to fit the coasters. Then lay the silhouette over each circle to get it into location. Use the slice tool to trim the silhouette to the right shape.

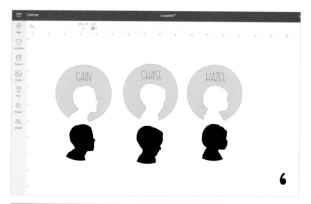

6. You should be left with a bunch of silhouettes for your coaster designs and circles with the silhouettes cut out of them. You do NOT want to delete the circle in this case. To each circle, we need to add some writing. I used a writing font to add a name to each of my coasters. Pick both the circle and the name and attach them together.

7. Be sure that your circles and your silhouettes are two different colors then click "make it." You should see two different mats. One with circles that have text written on them and one with silhouettes. Be sure to mirror both of these mats. Then click "continue" and pick the Infusible Ink sheet setting on your Cricut machine. Cut both sheets of Infusible Ink. Insert an Infusible Ink pen when prompted to draw the names on the sheet.

8. Be sure to preheat your EasyPress or heat press according to the Cricut Heat Guide. Cut the circles out of the larger sheet with scissors, then bend to crack the cut lines. Remove the outside portion of each coaster design. Repeat with the silhouettes. Use tweezers for weeding if needed. Then peel each silhouette from the backing paper and put it into place on each of the circles.

9. Clean the coaster surface with a lint roller, then apply the design, ink side down, on the surface. Since the design is solid at this point, the sticky liner is not going to hold it into place. Use heat resistant tape to hold everything so it will not move.

10. Repeat for all of the coasters you are making, as you can press them all at once. Add white cardstock to your EasyPress mat, then put the coasters face down on the mat. These ceramic coasters are pressed face down. You always want to read the instructions on the manufacturer's website for each sublimation blank. This is just one example where there is something odd that needs to happen to get a good final product.

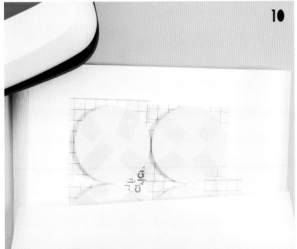

11. Add butcher paper over the coasters then put your EasyPress on top. You don't even have to push down with these. Just put the Easy-Press in place and don't move it until the time is up. Once the timer goes off, lift the Easy-Press straight up to remove. You will want to let these cool for 5 to 10 minutes minimum before touching. The ceramic coasters will burn you! Once cool, remove the paper to reveal your gorgeous design!

These cute silhouette coasters are perfect for moms and grandmas on any holiday! This is a great example of the proper way to layer Infusible Ink. Using this method means you only press once, which will eliminate a lot of possible issues.

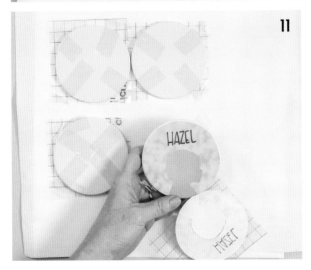

STENCILING

There are many ways to use your Cricut machine to make a stencil. From reusable stencils to one-time use versions, you can add designs to tons of different surfaces. Why stencil instead of using vinyl or HTV? On some projects, I like a painted look, and, in some situations, stenciling will last much longer. Either way, give stenciling a try with your Cricut!

STENCILING BASICS

MATERIALS FOR STENCILING

Let's take a look at the options for materials that can be used for making a stencil on your Cricut:

- **Removable and permanent vinyl:** Literally any vinyl you have on hand can be used to make a quick one-time-use stencil for painting on fabric, wood, glass and more. You can even use this material to make a temporary silkscreen.

- **Stencil vinyl:** Technically this is the vinyl that you want for all of your stencil making, and it does work better than the vinyl options above. You will get less bleed with this adhesive stencil material but it is still only for single-use applications.

- **Freezer paper:** If you want to stencil on fabric, this is the best material out there! I keep this on hand at all times and stencil a variety of fabrics with it.

- **Stencil film:** This Mylar® material is for cutting reusable stencils on your Cricut machine. You can purchase it in 12 x 12–inch (30.5 x 30.5–cm) sheets and make large stencils for walls, furniture and so much more.

- **Cardstock:** In a pinch, I have used cardstock as a quick and easy stencil for a project. Although I don't recommend this, it definitely can save you when you don't have any other materials.

- **Heat transfer vinyl:** HTV makes a great permanent silkscreen that you can use over and over again. If you think you need to make many of one thing over a period of time, screen printing may be the way to go.

WHICH STENCILS ARE REUSABLE?

If you just need to make one of something, any method of stenciling will work. However, there may be times when you would like to reuse your stencil over a large area or even over several projects. Really there are only two ways to make a reusable stencil with your Cricut. Those are cutting stencil film and making a silkscreen with HTV.

You can use a spray adhesive for stencil film to make it adhere to your surface, then wash it off and store it for use at a later time. I find that these can last a really long time when properly cared for. You will want to consider using registration marks when cutting if you want to use a stencil like this over a large area.

Screen printing is a more advanced craft that has a learning curve; however, it is really great when you need to make a lot of the same thing. HTV can be used to make a silkscreen in this case, and then you can wash and reuse it over time for as many projects as you need to create.

DESIGN CONSIDERATIONS

When making a temporary stencil, design isn't too important, as you can apply your vinyl with transfer tape just as you have in previous projects. However, if you are making a stencil with something like stencil film, you need to consider keeping things like the centers of letters or even cutouts in place. A stencil font is a great option for lettering. For other design elements, you can add a thin line or two between the outside of the stencil and your inner piece. These are often referenced as bridges. In the end, you want your stencil film to be one piece that can be placed and then moved to another location.

SURFACES THAT WORK WELL FOR STENCILING

There are so many things you can stencil. While smooth surfaces work best for stenciling, you can find tips and tricks for rough surfaces as well. Here are a few of my favorite surfaces:

- Fabric
- Wood
- Walls
- Floors
- Paper
- Metal
- Cork
- Glass
- And so much more!

STENCILING TOOLS

There are special tools to consider getting when working with a stencil. Here are a few of my favorites:

- **Stencil adhesive:** This is a spray adhesive that is repositionable and a must for stencils cut from the Mylar stencil film.

- **Pouncer or stencil brush:** I don't stencil anything without this type of brush on hand. They make it so much easier to get that clean look when stenciling any surface.

- **Small foam roller:** If you have a large stencil, you may want to consider rolling instead of using a stencil brush.

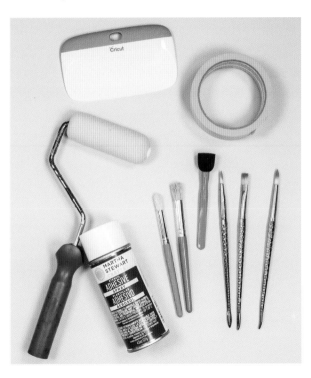

- **Painter's tape:** Use this to hold your stencil in place and to add some extra protection around the edges from excess paint.

- **Scraper:** This helps to apply vinyl stencils to your surface so that you get the best bond possible.

- **Paintbrushes:** You may need to use these to clean up around the edges of your project at times and to fill in some of those bridges that are keeping your stencil as one piece.

- **Cleaner:** You will want to make sure your surface is clean and dry. For hard surfaces especially, I recommend rubbing alcohol to remove all oils from the surface.

PAINT AND INK OPTIONS

Now that you have your tools of the trade, you will also want to pick up the paint of your choice to complete your project. Here are a few options:

- **Acrylic paint:** This is great for stenciling but you will need to use a stencil brush and remove most of the paint from your brush before application. You don't want the liquid to seep under the edges of your stencil.

- **Spray paint:** This can be a great option for some applications, but you will want to protect the area around your stencil well, as overspray can be a huge issue. Apply in several light coats to avoid as much bleed as possible.

- **Fabric paint or ink:** For any fabric project, you want to be sure to pick a paint that is intended for use on fabric. I would also caution you to follow all instructions, as many of these paints need to be heat set. If you are screen printing, look for inks that are made for that process for the best results.

- **Etching cream:** Although not a paint, glass etching cream is one of my favorite things to use with a stencil. Add an etched design to glass surfaces for a sophisticated-looking gift idea.

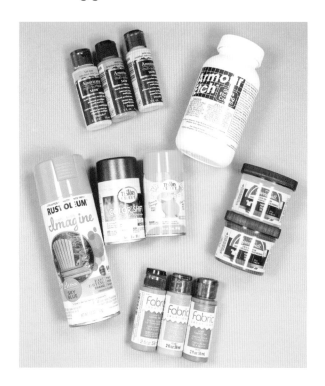

STENCILING TIPS AND TRICKS

I find stenciling both rewarding and frustrating. I have picked up several tips and tricks over the years, but I still feel like I have so much more to learn. I recommend starting with a small project and working your way up to a larger one to build your skills as well as your confidence. Be sure to follow these tips and tricks when starting out as well.

- Stenciling is easiest on a smooth surface. Although you can find methods for textured surfaces, I definitely recommend something smooth for your first project.

- When stenciling over a large surface, be sure to level or straighten your design and plan accordingly.

- Always add an adhesive to the back of a Mylar stencil before applying it to your surface. A stencil adhesive works to hold your stencil in place and keep paint from seeping underneath.

- Seal your stencil before you begin painting. I like to add one coat of the base color to my stencil if possible, then add on the color I want to paint. This allows the base color to seep into any areas of my stencil and seal them off before I begin. Stenciling on stained wood? You can do the same thing with a thin coat of Mod Podge as your first layer.

- Always use a stencil brush and paint from the top down. Do not paint from side to side when stenciling. Add your paint in an up and down motion to prevent pushing paint under the edges of your stencil.

- Do not get too much paint on the brush. Stenciling works best with a brush that is fairly dry, adding light coats on top of each other to get your desired look. Excess paint will run under your stencil and cause bleeding. Offload your brush if needed onto some paper towels to remove excess paint.

- Start painting at the edges of your stencil and work your way toward the center. This will prevent pushing paint under the edges.

- Mask off any areas of your stencil that you don't want to paint in the first pass. This is especially important if you are using more than one color.

- Allow your paint to dry for a few minutes before lifting the stencil. This will prevent any wet paint on the edges from getting on your project.

- After lifting your stencil, touch-ups may be needed and that is okay! You will have some mistakes but hopefully only a few. You will also want to paint in any bridged areas of your stencil to give it a more finished appearance once complete.

- Wash your reusable stencils after your project is complete and dry them before storing. You will also want to wash them off often if reusing over a large area, as paint can build up.

- Practice, practice, practice! It is the only way to get good at stenciling on any surface. However, I would also encourage you to embrace some imperfections. Stenciling is intended to give a hand-painted look that is rarely perfect in appearance.

MAKING YOUR DESIGN PERMANENT

Because you are working with paint, your design can wear on certain surfaces. If you are painting on a surface that will be used frequently or outdoors, consider a sealer. I usually use a sealer on furniture, floors and anything else that may see some wear.

When stenciling fabric, be sure to check the instructions on your bottle of paint or ink. Most require some sort of heat setting to make them permanent in the wash. Once the heat setting is complete, I find this method to be a durable way to add designs.

Now let's make a few projects using some of the methods described in this chapter. Start small with an easy project and work your way up to stenciling some furniture with a Stenciled Table Top (page 144).

ETCHED WINE GLASSES

Level: Beginner

Machine requirements: Any Cricut machine

Skills: Using stencil vinyl, glass etching, weeding boxes

Challenge: Want a more permanent label? Add etching to glass jars or canisters for a unique addition to your kitchen.

Supplies Needed

Stencil vinyl (you can also use permanent vinyl for this one)

Light grip (blue) Cricut mat

Fine point blade

Gloves

Wine glasses

Rubbing alcohol

Transfer tape (optional)

Scraper

Painter's tape

Glass etching cream

Paintbrush

Water

Glass etching is a simple way to start with stenciling, as it is fairly easy and forgiving. Here I am etching glasses, but you can try other pieces as well. Be aware that some glass will not etch. The general rule is that the higher the quality of glass, the less likely it is to etch with this method.

1. Upload the glass etching SVG file to Cricut Design Space (see page 55 for uploading help). Add it to your canvas and resize as needed. You will want to add a box around your design that is fairly large. This will help you to mask off your glass from excess etching cream. Want to randomly place these around your glass? Ungroup the file and move the stars around the mat, then draw boxes around each one. This works better for a more rounded surface. Attach each box to the stars.

Pro Tip: *You can also use this type of weeding box for regular vinyl projects to aid in weeding and even locating your design.*

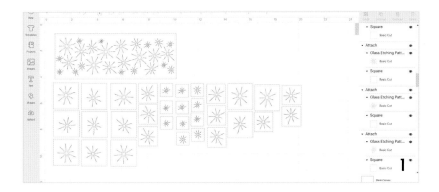

(continued)

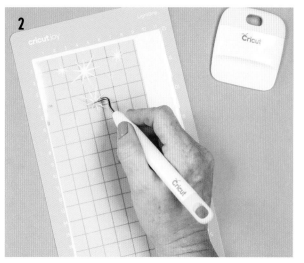

2. Click "make it" and use the basic cutting instructions on page 26 to cut the stencil vinyl. There is no need to mirror your design when cutting this material. For this material, you want to weed a bit differently. When stenciling, you want to remove everything that you want to be applied to your surface. So, you will leave the outside as well as the centers of any letters.

3. Once you start applying the vinyl, be sure to wear gloves. The oils from your hands can affect the etching cream. Clean the glass well with rubbing alcohol before starting. Use transfer tape if desired to move your design to your glass. Be sure to rub the vinyl down really well with a scraper.

4. Add tape around the outer edge of your design. Any place that your etching cream touches your glass, it will etch.

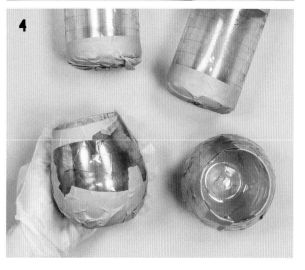

5. Apply your etching cream with a paintbrush in a thick coat. I like to brush in all four directions to make sure I have applied the cream to the entire stencil.

6. Allow the etching cream to sit according to the directions on your bottle. This will vary depending on the brand. Once the time is complete, you can put excess cream back in the bottle. Then rinse the remainder off with some water.

7. Remove the stencil from your glass and your project is complete. The glass etching is completely permanent on the surface.

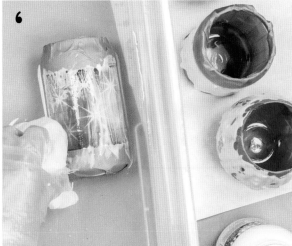

STENCILED TABLE TOP

Level: Intermediate

Machine requirements: Any Cricut machine (though using the Joy would be hard for a project this large)

Skills: Making a reusable stencil, stenciling with multiple colors, sealing

Challenge: Try using one of the SVGs provided for this book to stencil another surface like a wood sign. Remember that you will need to add bridges to design elements when using stencil film.

Supplies Needed

Stencil film

Medium grip (green) Cricut mat

Fine point blade

Table top or other furniture for painting

Stencil adhesive

Painter's tape

Acrylic paint (in the colors of your choice)

Mod Podge (optional)

Stencil brush

Sealer

Paintbrush

Making a reusable stencil is great for a ton of different project ideas. From stenciling furniture to walls and more, be sure to pick up some Mylar stencil film and give a project like this a try. Here I am stenciling on a table top, but you can use this same idea on a wall or something smaller, like a tray.

1. I used the hexagon shapes in Cricut Design Space to create a look that I liked. Make sure the design fits on the stencil film you will be cutting. Also, if you have any elements like letters that have a center, you will need to add rectangles or thick lines as bridges and weld those to the letter in order to get a stencil that will work correctly. Be sure to attach everything together before clicking "make it."

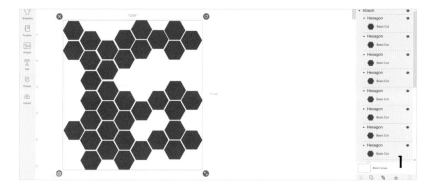

(continued)

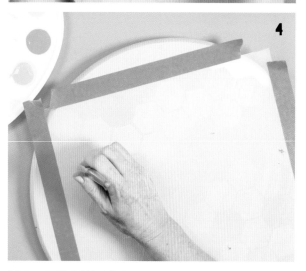

2. There is no need to mirror your cuts. Pick stencil film as your material and place the material onto the mat. Then cut with your Cricut machine. Once the Cricut is done cutting, DO NOT eject the mat from the machine. Instead, lift the material slightly to make sure it is cut though. If it is, click the "unload" button and remove it from the machine. If it is not cut through, click the "go" button again for an additional cut. I find that some brands of this material need another pass or two to cut completely through. Carefully remove the stencil from the mat. Again, it should all be in one piece if you have made your design correctly.

3. Start with a pre-painted surface. Spray the back of your stencil with a stencil adhesive. Be sure to do a light coat and follow all directions on the product. Once the adhesive is dry and tacky, you can apply it to your project. Press the stencil down well so that you don't have any gaps.

4. Add tape around the edges of the stencil. Then add a light coat of your base color to the entire stencil and allow that to dry. This will seal the stencil and give you a more perfect appearance. If you are using a stained surface, use Mod Podge instead with a finish that matches the paint you are using.

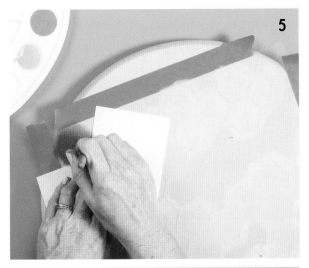

5. Once that is dry, start adding additional colors. Be sure to use a dry brush with just a little bit of paint. Start on the edges of each stencil opening and work your way to the middle. Use a stencil brush in an up and down motion. You can mask each of the other areas with more tape or use a few scrap pieces of paper to keep the paint in one area.

6. Once you are done painting, allow the final coat to dry for just a few minutes then pull away the stencil carefully. Allow the paint to dry completely at this point. You can come back after the paint has dried and perform any necessary touchups.

7. Once you are happy with the look of your painted surface, allow it to dry for at least 24 hours, then seal with a good quality sealer. This is important on furniture that will see a ton of wear or anything that will be outdoors. I used several coats of sealer on this table following the directions for application.

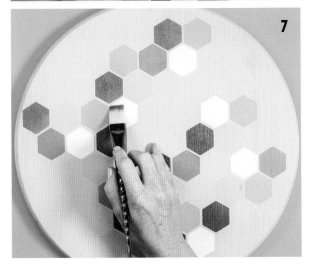

CUSTOM DOORMAT

Level: Advanced

Machine requirements: Any Cricut machine (though using the Joy would be hard for a project this large)

Skills: Using freezer paper, adding custom materials, using a large mat

Challenge: Freezer paper stenciling can be used on fabric projects as well. Try it on a shirt or a tea towel with fabric paint for your next project.

Supplies Needed

Freezer paper

Scissors

Light grip (blue) Cricut mat (using a 12 x 24–inch [30.5 x 61–cm] mat in a Maker or Explore series is best)

Fine point blade

Coir doormat

Cardboard

Iron

Painter's tape

Copy paper

Spray paint

Freezer paper is my absolute favorite way to stencil on any fabric surface. However, this coir doormat is a great surface as well! This method uses freezer paper along with spray paint to create a doormat that is all your own. The coir is also really forgiving for stenciling.

I. Add the text of your choice to Cricut Design Space. Be sure to resize to fit your Cricut mat and attach all text elements together.

2. There is no material setting for freezer paper in Design Space, but you can make your own. On the home page, click on the three lines in the upper left to drop down the menu and you will see "manage custom materials." This will only work if your machine is on and connected. I like to start with the settings for copy paper when cutting freezer paper (to see them, click "edit" beside the material).

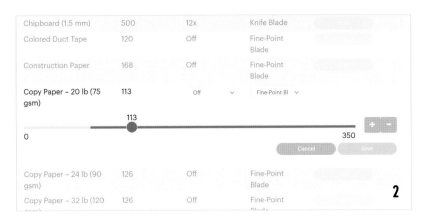

(continued)

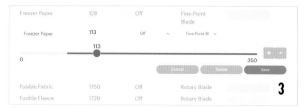

| Freezer Paper | 128 | Off | Fine-Point Blade |
| Freezer Paper | 113 | Off | Fine-Point Bl |

113

0   350

Cancel   Delete   Save

| Fusible Fabric | 1750 | Off | Rotary Blade |
| Fusible Fleece | 1739 | Off | Rotary Blade |

3

4

5

3. Then scroll all the way to the bottom and click "add new material." Add the same settings here as for copy paper with the description as "freezer paper." You can also come back here at any time and increase or decrease the pressure if your Cricut is cutting too shallow or too deep.

4. Go back to your canvas and click "make it." You don't have to mirror this material and it should show on a large mat. Now you can pick the custom material you just made from your material list. Remember that ONLY freezer paper will work for this project. Any other type of paper will not work. Cut the paper with scissors to the size of your Cricut mat and put the shiny side down.

5. Cut your freezer paper using the fine point blade. Then remove all of the pieces that you want to be painted. I will show you how to apply those later.

6. Put your doormat on a large piece of cardboard. It will be easier to move outdoors if you do this now. You can also just take your iron outside where you will be painting and do this all at once. Preheat your iron and locate your design on the coir door mat. Start pressing into place with your iron.

7. The iron will heat up the adhesive on the shiny side of the paper. This adhesive is just strong enough to adhere to the material for painting. It will not be a very strong bond. It only needs a few seconds of a press to hold. Once your outside piece is in place, remove the centers of your letters from your mat and apply each one with an iron. Repeat until you have the entire stencil on the doormat.

8. Apply painter's tape and copy paper around the entire mat. You don't want any overspray on your surface.

9. Lift the entire thing up by the cardboard and move outside to paint. Shake your can of spray paint well and hold it above your stencil, keeping the can perpendicular to the mat. Apply the paint in several light coats one right after the other. Be sure to do this on a day when it is not windy.

10. Once you have enough coats to get the look you want, allow the paint to dry 5 to 10 minutes, then carefully peel everything back. Allow the doormat to dry completely, and it is ready to add to your outdoor décor! I have made several doormats this way and used them for many months with no issues. Just be sure to use a spray paint that is rated for outdoor use.

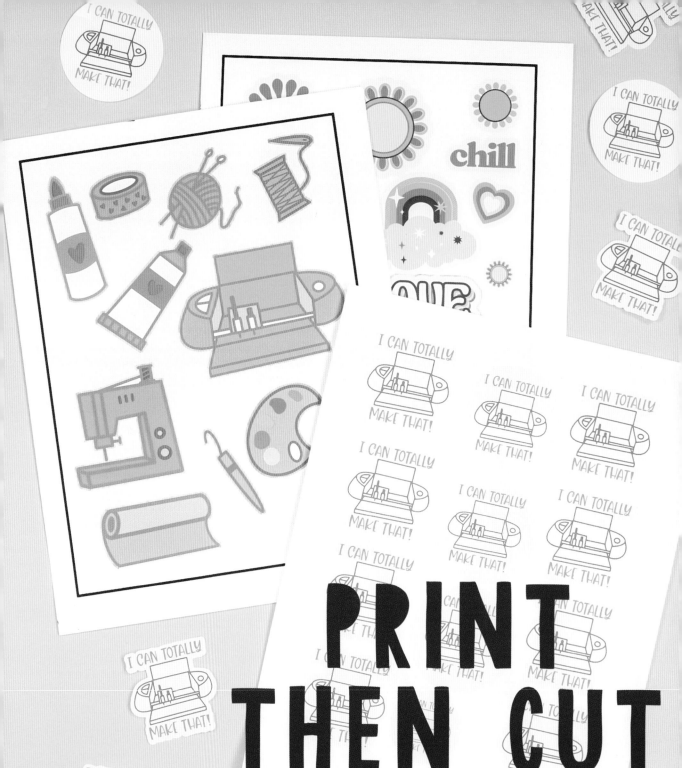

PRINT THEN CUT

What exactly is Print Then Cut? Your Cricut Explore series or Maker series machines can communicate with your printer through Cricut Design Space. That allows you to print something, then cut around what you printed with your Cricut machine. This opens up even more crafting opportunities with photos, stickers and so much more! At this time, Print Then Cut is not available on the mobile application.

PRINT THEN CUT BASICS

MACHINES THAT WORK WITH PRINT THEN CUT

The Cricut Joy machine will not work with Print Then Cut, but the Explore and Maker machines have this function. However, not all of the machines are the same. With the Explore series, the Explore Air 2 and earlier have the old sensor design, while the Explore 3, Maker and Maker 3 all have an upgraded sensor. That means that these three machines can Print Then Cut on colored paper. The earlier machines are only able to see the registration marks on white paper.

Any printer that is hooked up to your computer will work with Print Then Cut. I recommend clicking "use system dialogue box" on the Print Then Cut screen and altering your settings. I usually choose "best quality," turn off any fast printing modes and change the paper type to something similar to what I am printing on.

PRINTABLE MATERIALS

You may think that Print Then Cut is only for plain paper, but there are so many more options on the market for printable materials that you can use with your machine.

- **Cardstock and paper:** Just be sure you either purchase the size that will fit in your printer or trim it down to fit before printing.

- **Printable vinyl:** Print your own vinyl designs and use them for a variety of projects. I use this material for stickers as well. It is my favorite printable material.

- **Sticker paper:** There is a wide variety of sticker papers on the market, from holographic to glitter to glossy and more. You can also look for options that say waterproof; however, my favorite waterproof versions use a laminate over the top for protection.

- **Printable HTV and t-shirt transfers:** You can print things to add to shirts directly from your home printer! These materials are easy to use; however, I find they do not last as long as regular HTV and Infusible Ink.

- **Printable fabric:** These stiff fabric sheets can actually be cut on the Explore and Maker series machines. The next chapter covers fabric crafting, but you may keep these in mind.

- **Shrink plastic:** If you are looking to make cute plastic crafts on your Cricut machine, be sure to give this material a try. Add your design to printable shrink film, cut with your Cricut, then shrink to size in an oven. These may remind you of your childhood, but you can definitely make stunning crafts with this product.

- **Printable magnet sheets:** Make magnets as easily as stickers with your Explore or Maker machine.

- **Waterslide decals:** Add a printed image to glass or wood. These are not made for applications with heavy use, but they are great for decorative purposes.

- **Tattoo paper:** Temporary tattoos are fun for kids, or use this paper to make crafts as well!

I am sure there are even more products on the market. You can do so much more than make stickers with the Print Then Cut function on your Cricut machine.

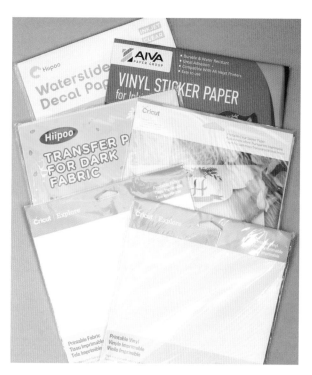

HOW DOES PRINT THEN CUT WORK?

When you make a design in Cricut Design Space, you set it to be a printed design. Then when you click "make it," you will see it on the mat with a black registration box around it. The next screen will prompt you to print the page first before cutting. The registration box will print along with the design on your home printer.

Your Cricut then uses that black box to locate the cuts. When you add your mat to your machine and press "go," you may notice that a light comes on inside your machine. The machine will then go around the box and try to find those black lines. This makes the registration box extremely important! That is the only thing that tells your Cricut where the cuts should be located.

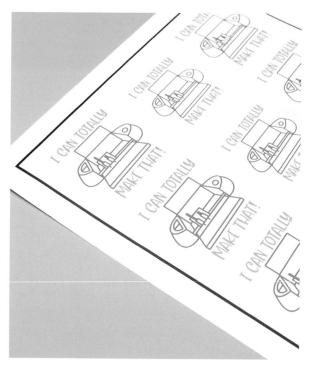

PRINT THEN CUT SIZE

There is a maximum size for Print Then Cut designs that you will need to keep in mind. Currently, the maximum size is 6.75 x 9.25 inches (17.1 x 23.5 cm). This allows room around a standard sheet of paper for the registration box and the machine to read those marks. This is a limitation with the feature, but I have made many things using Print Then Cut while staying within this size.

FLATTENING YOUR DESIGNS

"Flatten" is the term Cricut uses to describe turning any project from a cut to something that is printed. You can use flatten on shapes, text and more. For images, you want to upload those as a Print Then Cut file using the options during that process.

When flattening, be sure to consider what the cut lines will be. For instance, if you were to flatten just a single word, each of the letters would be cut out after printing. You may find it more useful to flatten to another object or shape. You can put a white rectangle behind that same word, pick both the shape and the text, then click "flatten." Now your Cricut will cut around the outside of the rectangle, leaving your text all as one piece. There are a variety of ways to do this and a few of those are covered within this chapter.

WHEN TO USE BLEED

When using Print Then Cut, you will be given the option to turn on bleed when printing. Bleed will give a faint outline around your shape in the same color as your printed design. This gives some room for error with the cuts and often results in a better Print Then Cut result. However, the printed page will look really odd with the bleed on. Remember, most of this excess will be cut away!

I like to use bleed when I have a solid color or simple pattern for my outside design. Busy patterns often don't work well with this function and I usually don't use it for printing photographs.

KISS CUT VERSUS THROUGH CUT

When cutting HTV or vinyl, you always want a kiss cut, as you want your backing paper to stay in one piece. With Print Then Cut stickers, you may not want a kiss cut. Some people want the backing paper left as one piece to easily peel the stickers for use. Others like to cut all the way through the backing paper to have individual stickers with their own backing paper. It is all about personal preference, and you can do both on your Cricut machine.

For a kiss cut, I always select the cut setting for the material type that I am using. For example, printable vinyl cuts great on the vinyl setting on my machine and I get a perfect kiss cut for my stickers. If I wanted a through cut instead, I would change to a cardstock setting so that my Cricut would cut deeper into the material. You might have to experiment a bit to find the correct setting for the printable material that you are using.

PRINT THEN CUT CALIBRATION

Your Cricut machine can be calibrated to improve the location of the cuts with the Print Then Cut function. This will not fix all Print Then Cut issues. I have more troubleshooting tips in the next section; however, calibration is a good place to start.

Click the three lines in the upper left-hand corner and click "calibration." Then pick Print Then Cut and walk through the steps on the screen. You can often get a better cut location by running the calibration on your machine.

PRINT THEN CUT TROUBLESHOOTING

While Print Then Cut is an awesome feature, it can also be challenging at times. Here are a few of my tips and tricks for getting the best results possible.

- Make sure you are only using white paper on a Cricut Explore Air 2 or earlier machine. This really does mean only white! The early machines will not even work with kraft paper.

- Remember to stay within the size restrictions of 6.75 x 9.25 inches (17.1 x 23.5 cm).

- Be sure to put the paper on the mat in the same orientation as it is shown on your screen in Cricut Design Space.

- Print Then Cut is best on materials that have a matte finish. Any shine to the finish may cause the sensor to not read correctly. The trick for this is to cover the registration box on any glossy materials with clear matte finish tape. This will often fix this issue and correct the location of your cuts.

- For materials with a laminate, only add the laminate to the area inside of the registration box. This will prevent the sensor from misreading the box due to the glossy nature of the laminate.

- Try different lighting in your room if your sensor doesn't seem to be reading correctly. Adding or even taking away light may help.

- Run calibration on Print Then Cut if you continue to have issues with the cut location.

- Add bleed to your design if you can to give yourself some more room for error when it comes to cut location.

- Add an offset around your design in white. This will give you a bit more wiggle room for cuts and give your products a more professional appearance.

- Make sure there isn't any debris or dust on your Print Then Cut sensor blocking it from reading your paper.

- Make sure your black box is printed completely and is a dark black. You may need to adjust your printer settings or add ink.

- Be sure your mat is pushed all the way over to the left when loading for calibration as well as for Print Then Cut.

- As a last resort, call Cricut customer service if you continue to have issues with your Print Then Cut sensor. There can be cases where you need a replacement.

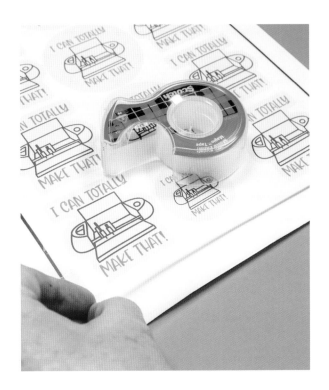

BEYOND THE BASICS

Start with the projects in this book, then move on to some more challenging Print Then Cut crafts. I recommend working your way through the list of printable materials and seeing how many of those you can turn into amazing creations for your home. I think that you will find that Print Then Cut is something that you will use in a variety of cases.

PRINT THEN CUT STICKERS

Level: Beginner

Machine requirements: Explore or Maker Machines Only

Skills: Print then cut, flatten

Challenge: Design more stickers with images, text, shapes, files from this book and so much more!

Supplies Needed

Printable vinyl or sticker paper

Printer

Fine point blade

Light grip (blue) Cricut mat

Everyone loves stickers! Whether making crafty stickers like these for fun or using this same process to make gift tags, you will find a reason to use a few stickers around your home.

1. Use the same file you uploaded for the Crafty HTV Shirt (page 93) by clicking "upload," then "add to canvas." Resize the design to make stickers in any size. Change the colors of each layer to be whatever you would like them to be. You can now add an offset (page 98) or a shape to complete your sticker.

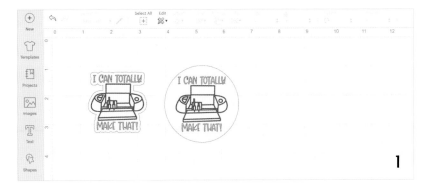

2. It is time to flatten the design for Print Then Cut. Pick all of the layers for your sticker and click "flatten" in the bottom right toolbar. You should see the layer change to Print Then Cut.

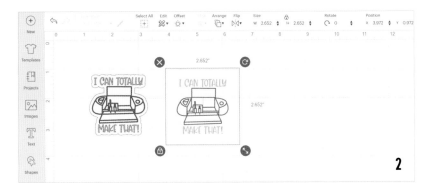

(continued)

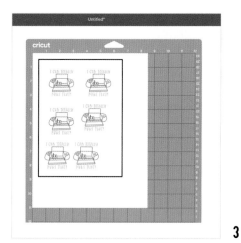

3

4

3. You can click "make it" from here and just make a few stickers if you would like. I tend to make a full sheet of printable projects so as to not waste any material. There are a few ways that you can do this. One way is to click "make it" then change the project copies in the box at the top left of the screen to fill the page.

4. This doesn't always result in a full page. To get around this, you can also make a sticker sheet manually on your canvas. Start by adding a 6.75 x 9.25 inch (17.1 x 23.5 cm) box. You can then duplicate your stickers and rearrange them to make the most out of the printable area that you have. I like this method, as I can make copies that are smaller in size to fill some of the unused areas.

5. Once you have it the way you like it, delete the rectangle. Then pick all of your stickers and click "attach." Now when you click "make it," you will have an entire sheet of stickers that is as full as you can get it.

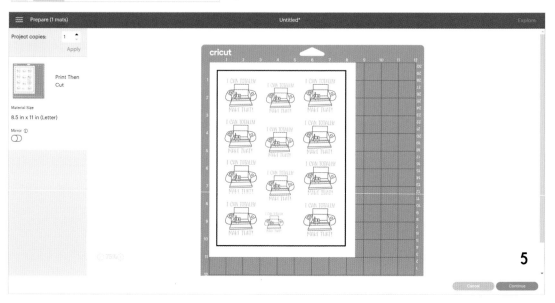

5

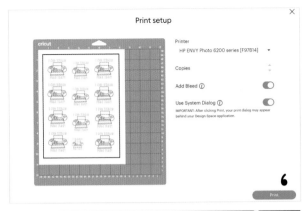

6. Click "continue" then click "send to printer." You can send it to any printer that is connected to your computer. Here I am choosing to add bleed and also to use my system dialogue box. I like to change the settings for my prints so I use the dialogue box each time. Each printer will be different; however, I like to choose the best quality and a matte paper setting for this type of printable vinyl.

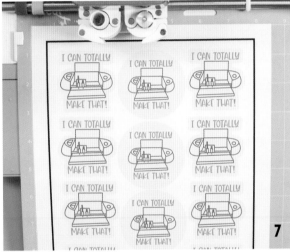

7. Print your design onto the printable vinyl or the sticker paper of your choice. Please note that thicker sticker papers will not work on all printers. I prefer the thinner printable vinyl for my projects. Then add that printed sheet to your mat. Remember that this must be in the same orientation on your mat as it is shown in Cricut Design Space. Add your mat to your Cricut machine. Pick the material setting of your choice in Design Space. This will depend on if you want a kiss cut or a through cut (see Kiss Cut Versus Through Cut, page 156).

8. Once your stickers are cut, remove the sheet or individual stickers from the mat. You can remove the excess around the outer edge for a sheet of stickers. All that is left to do is to use your stickers on the surface of your choice!

CHIPBOARD PUZZLE

Level: Advanced

Machine requirements:
Maker Machines Only

Skills: Knife blade, flipping objects

Challenge: Make a second puzzle with the photo of your choice instead of the flattened design used here.

Supplies Needed

Printable vinyl or sticker paper

Printer

Chipboard (1.5 mm is perfect for puzzles)

Strong grip (purple) Cricut mat

Brayer

Painter's tape

Knife blade

Craft knife

Self-healing cutting mat

You can use your Maker to cut a thick chipboard to make puzzles of all types. Here I am using this idea to make a birth announcement, but you can use any image or text of your choice in place of this design. The knife blade does not work on the mobile app so you will need a computer for this project.

1. Upload the puzzle file from cricuthandbook.com to Cricut Design Space. You can resize it if you would like. Remember that the maximum width is 6.75 inches (17.1 cm) for Print Then Cut. Make a second copy of the puzzle and start adding your design over the top. I used a variety of text and shapes for my design. To get an exact mirrored copy of any design, click the design then pick "flip" in the upper toolbar. In this case, I flipped horizontally.

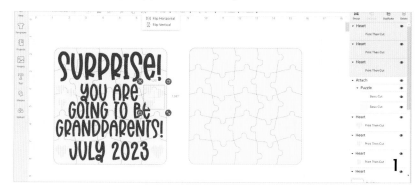

2. Pick the second copy of your puzzle and remove the inner cut lines. Then pick the entire design as well as the outer puzzle square and click "flatten." This will make a Print Then Cut design for the front of your puzzle.

(continued)

SURPRISE! YOU ARE GOING TO BE GRANDPARENTS! JULY 2023

3. On the first copy of your puzzle, remove the outer cut edge. Then choose both the Print Then Cut design and the puzzle and align in the center. Then attach them together. This will put the cut lines of your puzzle on your printed design.

4. Click "make it" then print your design for the puzzle onto the printable vinyl. Do not cut the vinyl at this point! Peel the backing from the entire sheet of vinyl and apply to the chipboard.

5. Then add the chipboard sheet to the strong grip mat. Press it down well with the brayer and add painter's tape to the entire outer edge. Be sure to only cover a small portion of the chipboard and do not cover any of the registration box. Move your star wheels all the way over to the right and add the knife blade to your Maker machine. Choose the chipboard setting that is the same thickness as what you are using.

6. Press the "go" button when prompted to start the cut. You will see the Maker read the registration box first; then it will begin to cut your puzzle. Cutting with the knife blade is a long process. After the first pass, Design Space will tell you approximately how long it will take. The knife blade may pick up and spin occasionally as it cuts. This is okay! It is part of the process and you should not be concerned.

7. For chipboard, I like to start checking my cuts around the halfway mark. Hit the "pause" button on the machine and lift the edge to see if it is cut through. The curves and tight corners will cut through last; however, the knife blade does have the power to cut through your mat and damage your machine. Always use caution when cutting with this tool.

8. If your material is not cut though, press "go" to resume cutting. If it is cut through, you can press the arrow button to remove the mat from the machine. Check using this method every few passes. Once the cut is complete, do not eject your mat! You want to check the cuts again at the end, as there is a possibility that the chipboard is not cut all the way through. If it isn't, click the "go" button again without unloading your mat to go another pass. You can repeat this as many times as needed as long as you do not unload your mat.

9. When the cuts are through, eject the mat and start removing your puzzle pieces from the mat. I like to remove the outer scrap first, then each puzzle piece. You can finish any cuts with the craft knife if you have a small area that did not cut all the way through. Then your puzzle is done and ready to give away or keep for yourself!

FABRIC

Working with a variety of fabrics on your Cricut Explore or Maker can be a fun way to stretch your machine's capabilities. One of my favorite materials to cut with my machine is felt. You can cut other fabrics as well and even cut pieces for your sewing projects!

FABRIC CRAFTING BASICS

FABRIC TYPES FOR CUTTING

There are so many fabrics on the market; however, not all of them can be cut with all machines. The Cricut Joy cannot cut fabric at all. However, the Explore and Maker can cut a wide range of different types. Let's take a look at some of the options:

- **Felt:** There are so many different varieties of felt on the market. I find that only stiff felt cuts well on the Explore series. You can try adding interfacing to other types of felt but I have mixed results with that on the Explore. The Maker, however, has been able to cut just about any felt that I have tried.

- **Bonded fabric:** This is fabric that has interfacing applied to the back. The interfacing makes the fabric stiffer and easier to cut for some machines. You can use any type of interfacing that will work with the project you have in mind. This type of fabric is primarily cut on the Explore series but the Maker machines can cut bonded fabric as well.

- **Plain fabric:** All other types of fabric will need to be cut on a Maker machine. The Explore just does not have the capability to cut fabric without an interfacing on the back. The Maker can cut hundreds of different fabric types, so the sky is really the limit.

TYPES OF INTERFACING

Although any brand of interfacing will work for your projects, there are several different types on the market. Which works best for Cricut projects? You do want to always use a fusible interfacing that you can iron on to the back of the fabric. Here are a few you may consider:

- **No-sew:** Want to just iron on your appliques and move on to the next project? Then you will want a permanent interfacing that does not require you to sew the fabric after application.

- **Sewable:** If you would like to sew around the outside of your appliqué after it is applied, you will need an interfacing that allows for this. The same general methods apply for application as with the no-sew version, but the adhesive on this version allows you to easily sew through it.

For appliqué, my personal preference is interfacing with a double-sided adhesive. This allows you to secure it to the back of your fabric, cut it and then add the fabric to your project, all with a household iron. Double-sided fusible interfacing usually has a paper backing to make it easier to apply. You can also find single-sided interfacing that you can secure to the back of your fabric to give it body for cutting. This type is also used to provide structure to a project, such as a bag or purse. Choose the best option for the type of project you are working on.

Note: *Be sure to follow all instructions on your package of interfacing for both the application and the care directions.*

BLADES FOR CUTTING FABRIC

Primarily, you will use two different blades for cutting fabric on your Cricut machines.

- **Bonded fabric blade:** This blade is just the fine point blade in a pink housing. As with fabric scissors, you want one blade that is for cutting fabric only. The pink housing will allow you to keep this blade separate from the blades you use for cutting paper, vinyl and more. You can use this blade in the Explore or the Maker.

- **Rotary blade:** This blade is a small version of the rotary cutter you may have for cutting fabric by hand. It is for the Maker series only and cuts fabric like a dream. This is the only blade I use for fabric and felt on my Maker machine. I even use it if I want to cut bonded fabric on the Maker.

DESIGN CONSIDERATIONS

I find that small details do not cut well from fabric or felt with either the Explore or the Maker. Try to make your designs a bit larger for these materials. In addition, the rotary blade can dig into your mat on tight turns. Cricut recommends that all turns be at least 0.75 inch (1.9 cm) in diameter. I do not follow this rule completely. I find that my mat will still be sticky even with a few scars from the rotary blade.

FABRIC CRAFTING TOOLS

As with any other craft, you will need certain tools when working with fabrics. Here are a few of my favorites:

- Handheld rotary cutter
- Self-healing mat
- Ruler
- Brayer
- Tweezers
- Washable fabric pen
- Sewing machine
- Thread
- Pins
- Needles

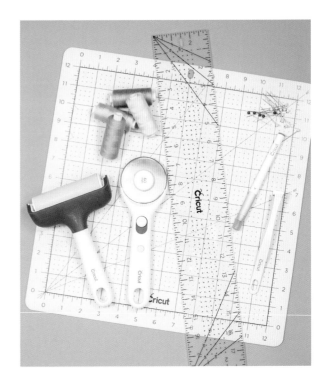

Not all of these tools will be needed for every project, and you may find that you do not need some at all. I always recommend picking up tools as you find that you need them to avoid having a ton of things that you never use.

PINK FABRIC MAT

There is a pink fabric mat that is great for cutting fabric of all types. I use it for most fabrics, including bonded fabric. Thicker fabrics may require a stronger grip mat. Thicker felts, flannels and other fuzzy material can definitely ruin your mat, as they will leave fibers in the adhesive. One trick is to use a light or medium grip mat with some transfer tape added to the adhesive. Then you can use the transfer tape to secure the material and protect the mat itself.

The adhesive of the pink fabric mat is different from any other mat. The oils from your hands can break down the material and cause your mat to be less sticky over time. Try to touch the mat's surface as little as possible. Also, clean the mat by using transfer tape to pull up any debris. Washing these mats with water does not work as well as the other types of mats.

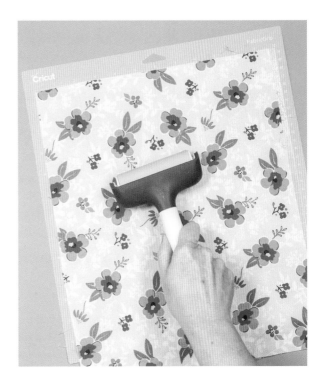

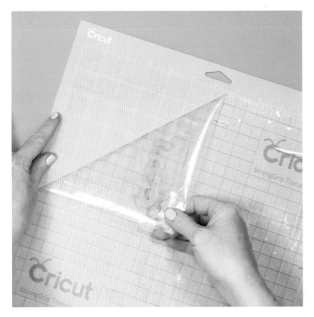

ADDING MATERIALS TO THE MAT

You can add your fabric to the mat right side up or down. If you are going to mark your pattern pieces with the washable fabric pen, you would want to put the right side down and mirror your design. If you just want to cut your fabric, adding it right side up works fine. For bonded fabric, I always add the material with the interfacing down on the mat. Put the material on the mat, then use a brayer over the entire surface to make sure it is down well. You can use the transfer tape hack mentioned (see "Pink Fabric Mat," above) for materials that shed.

CUT SETTINGS FOR FABRIC

Always pick the closest setting to the material that you will be cutting to start. You may find that this is not enough or too much pressure, and you can adjust from there. Remember that all fabrics will be different and each one may require a bit of experimentation to get the cuts just right.

FABRIC CUTTING TROUBLESHOOTING

Want your Cricut fabric projects to turn out great every single time? Take a look at the tips and tricks below for making the most out of your machine.

- Always press your material down well on the mat with a brayer. This is critical when cutting fabrics.

- Using one blade for all of your fabric projects will improve your cuts. Cutting paper and other materials can dull your blade and make cutting fabric much more difficult.

- You may find some fraying on the edges of your cut fabric pieces and that is okay. Just snip away any loose threads.

- Remove the fabric from your mat carefully. The adhesive on the mat can grab loose threads and unravel your fabric.

- You may find that the rotary blade skips a few threads when cutting. Just snip those when removing your material from the mat. If you find, however, that it is skipping larger areas, you may have a nick in the blade and it should be replaced.

- If you are having issues with a certain design, look at it and make sure it is not too detailed as per Design Considerations (page 168). You may need to add a chunkier font or make the entire thing larger.

- To prevent your rotary blade from digging into your mat, make the diameter of any turns larger.

BEYOND THE BASICS

Now that you know the basics of cutting fabric with your Cricut, try a few of these techniques to take your crafts to the next level!

- Convert sewing patterns to Cricut Design Space files. You can even use the washable fabric pen to add seam allowance marks and more.

- Use SnapMat on the iPad or iPhone to locate your cuts exactly on the mat and fussy cut your fabric for your projects.

- Expand beyond just store-bought fabric and cut upcycled materials as well. Denim, flannel and more materials from old clothing can be used to make creative projects.

FELT SUCCULENT WREATH

Level: Intermediate

Machine requirements: Explore or Maker Machines

Skills: Cutting felt, editing tools

Challenge: Use the flower and leaf designs from earlier in this book and cut those from felt as well.

Supplies Needed

Stiff felt (I am using the Cricut brand)

Medium grip (green) Cricut mat

Transfer tape (optional)

Brayer

Fine point blade, bonded fabric blade or rotary blade

Hot glue gun and hot glue

Silicone mat

EasyPress mat or pillow

Silicone finger tip

Scissors

Wreath form

Ribbon

Felt is one of my favorite things to cut with a Cricut. It is really versatile for a wide variety of projects and looks stunning once assembled. Here I am showing it off with some felt succulents on a wreath, but you can use these same skills to cut a variety of felt plants and flowers for your home's décor.

1. Upload the succulent shapes to Cricut Design Space. Resize as needed to fit your material or make the size of succulent that you want for your project. Remember to not make your projects too small, or they will not cut correctly.

(continued)

2. The Cricut felt brand works well directly on their mats, though you can add transfer tape to the mat to protect it from fibers. Just put the tape on the mat with the sticky side up and remove the backing paper. Then add your felt to the mat. Press the felt down well with a brayer.

3. Then cut on either your Explore or Maker machine. With the Maker, I like to use my rotary blade if possible. You can use your fine point or bonded fabric blade for the stiff felt, however. To change blades on any material, click "edit tools" in Design Space before loading your mat. This button will be highlighted if there are additional options. Once your pieces are cut, remove them from the mat. Save the scraps, as you will need a few of those for assembling the wreath later.

4. Use hot glue to assemble each succulent. Put your silicone mat over your EasyPress mat. Start with the bottom layer of the succulent and add glue to the center. Stack on the second layer and use the silicone fingertip to press down in the center while the glue cools, for a 3D appearance once complete.

5. Repeat with all of the layers in your design. Do not press as much on the top layer so the glue does not show through your felt.

6. Add hot glue to the back of the succulent, put the wreath form into place, then add a scrap piece and hold it in place while the glue cools. Repeat with all of your succulents to complete your wreath, then hang it up with some ribbon.

APPLIQUÉ ONESIE

Level: Intermediate

Machine requirements: Explore or Maker Machines Only

Skills: Using the bonded fabric blade

Challenge: Expand beyond just a onesie with this project. Add a chunky letter to a tote bag or even a design on a tea towel.

Supplies Needed

Fabric of your choice

Interfacing (see Types of Interfacing, page 167)

Fabric grip (pink) Cricut mat

Brayer

Fine point blade, bonded fabric blade or rotary blade

Iron

Onesie

Sewing machine (optional)

You can cut your own appliqués in any shape with your Cricut Explore or Maker machine. This is the perfect fabric crafting project for those who have an Explore, as bonded fabric makes this project super easy!

1. Use the skills from page 107 to find free images for the appliqués in Cricut Design Space. I found three images that I thought would work well.

2. Add the interfacing on the back of your fabric according to the package directions. Remember that you only need fabric the size of your appliqué but you will need some extra around the edges. I am using no-sew interfacing so I do not have to finish off the appliqué with a sewing machine once it is complete.

(continued)

3. Peel the paper from the back of the interfacing and place your material, interfacing side down, on the mat. I have cut material with the paper backing in place as well. I find that both ways work well. You can put multiple pieces on the mat at once using the same techniques as in Vinyl on a Tumbler (page 77). Press the material into your mat well with a brayer. Pick the bonded fabric setting on your machine and use your bonded fabric blade to cut the material.

Note: *You can click "edit tools" and change to the rotary blade if you are using the Maker. I actually recommend this, as the rotary blade cuts better in my opinion.*

4. Once the material is cut, remove the pieces from your mat. Apply the pieces to your onesie with an iron according to the package directions for the brand of interfacing that you are using. If you are using no-sew interfacing, your project is ready! If you used the version that must be sewed, you will need to stitch around the outer edge of the appliqué.

ZIPPER POUCH

Level: Intermediate

Machine requirements: Maker Machines Only

Skills: Using the rotary blade, patterns

Challenge: This project is just the beginning! Use these skills to create more simple sewing patterns right in Cricut Design Space.

Supplies Needed

Fabrics of your choice (one for the outer surface and one for the liner)

Printable HTV

Light grip (blue) Cricut mat

Fine point blade

Fabric grip (pink) Cricut mat

Brayer

Rotary blade

Heat transfer vinyl

Iron

Zipper

Pins

Sewing machine

Zipper foot

Sewing projects just got a little bit easier now that you have the Cricut Maker and the rotary blade. It is definitely my favorite tool for cutting fabric of all types. If you are looking for a precise way to cut your fabric crafts, the rotary blade is a must!

1. Draw 4 equal-sized rectangles in Cricut Design Space. I made mine 5 x 7 inches (12.7 x 17.8 cm), as my zippers are 8 inches (20.3 cm) long. You want your widest measurement to be shorter than the size of the zipper. Make two rectangles of one color and two of another color, as you will want to cut an outer fabric as well as a liner fabric.

2. You can also add text or another design to your mat that will be cut from HTV and added to the front. I used the skills in the Wood Door Hanger project (page 107) to find a few free images. I want to make the cactus from printable HTV, so let's add a pattern. First pull down the operation box in the top toolbar and choose Print Then Cut standard.

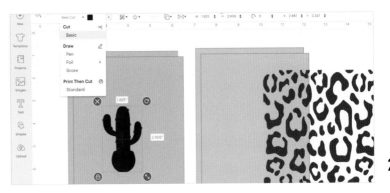

(continued)

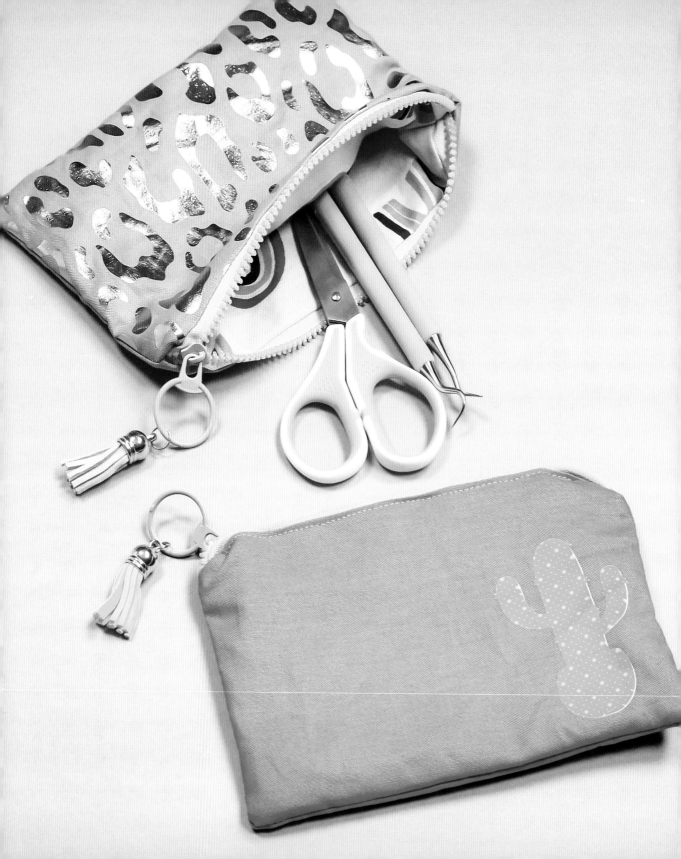

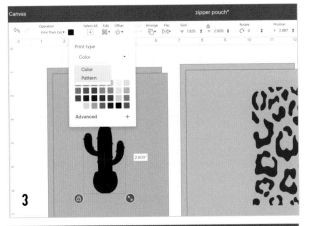

3.

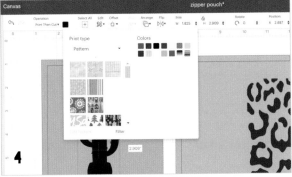

4.

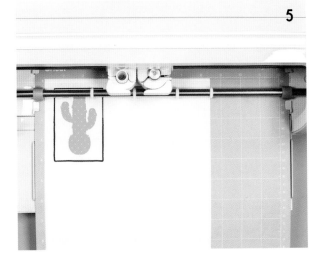

5

3. Then pick the color box next to the operation pull down and change from color to pattern.

4. Here you can scroll through the available patterns and even click "filter" to only look at a certain color. There is also an option for patterns on the upload screen if you have an image you want to upload there and use with this feature. Pick a pattern you like from the selection.

Pro Tip: You can click "edit pattern" and a dialogue box will appear that will allow you to alter the appearance.

5. Once you have your design, click "make it." Print the cactus onto printable HTV. I find this material to be much better than heat transfer sheets, so it is what I generally use. Follow all instructions that come with the brand of printable HTV that you are using. Add the material to the mat for cutting. Cut the printable HTV using the fine point blade and the Everyday Iron-On setting. This setting may or may not work for the brand of material that you are using. Be sure to do a small test cut.

6. Then remove the image from the backing for application to your fabric. Since this is a single piece, I will just remove and place it by hand. If you have a more complicated design, consider using a heat mask (see Heat Transfer Mask, page 86).

6

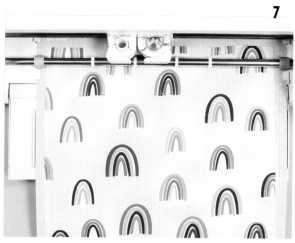

7

8

9

7. Add your material to the fabric grip mat without any backing on the fabric. I am cutting my fabric good side up so I don't have to mirror my design. Be sure to press down well with a brayer to adhere the fabric to the mat. Then use the rotary blade and the Maker to cut the pieces of fabric to size.

8. Remove the fabric pieces from the fabric grip mat using tweezers. Cut the regular HTV with the fine point blade. Be sure to mirror the design before cutting. Weed the HTV. Then press it to one side of your outer fabric. I also pressed the printable HTV design to the fabric for the second pouch. Be sure to cover it with a Teflon sheet or parchment paper when pressing.

9. Start with one piece of outer fabric and one piece of liner fabric with the right sides together. Add the zipper to the inside of this sandwich with the top of the zipper facing the outer fabric. Line up the edge of the zipper with the raw edges of the fabric. Pin into place if you would like.

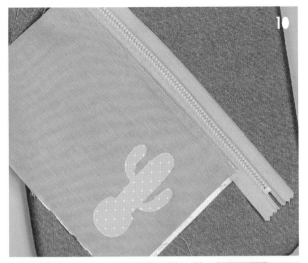

10. Add your zipper foot to your sewing machine and sew along the zipper. Flip the fabric over and pull back from the zipper. Press into place. Then use the sewing machine with the zipper foot to top stitch along the zipper.

11. Sandwich this sewn piece between the other outer and lining pieces. Your stack should be as follows: lining piece face up, sewn piece with zipper in place, then outer piece face down. The two outer fabrics and two lining fabrics will be touching and the right sides of each will be together. Pin into place if you would like.

12. Use the zipper foot to sew along the zipper on the opposite side. Turn the fabric pieces back to reveal the zipper and press. Top stitch the opposite side in the same manner as before.

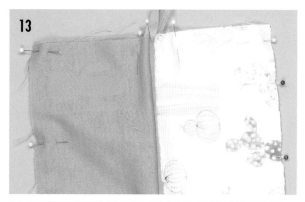

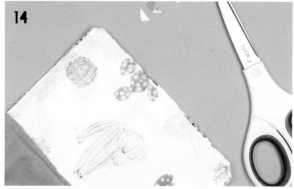

13. Be sure to open your zipper halfway. This is very important for turning your bag right side out. Put the lining and the outer fabric with the right sides together. Pin around the outside. Be sure that the zipper raw edges all face the lining side of your pouch.

14. Switch back to your regular sewing foot. Sew around the outside edge of your bag, leaving a 3- to 4-inch (7.5- to 10-cm) gap in the liner for turning. Cut off the zipper ends, then clip the corners. Make sure not to cut the stitching in the corners, just any excess fabric.

15. Reach through the hole that you left in the lining and turn the pouch right side out. This is where having that zipper halfway open is important. Be sure to turn out the corners as well.

16. Sew closed the hole you left in the liner. Put the liner back inside: You have a zipper pouch!

ACKNOWLEDGMENTS

As I wrap up this labor of love, I want to thank a few people who made this book possible. Without all of your support, I could never be where I am today.

First, a huge thank you to the entire team at Cricut for making amazing products and being the best to partner with over the years.

A huge thank you to the team at Page Street Publishing Co., not only for believing in me but also for allowing me to create the book of my dreams.

To my loving community of blog friends who continually keep me inspired and laughing, you are what keeps me going each day! This journey would be so lonely without you. A special thanks to Cori George, Heidi Kundin, Cheryl Spangenberg, Charynn Olsheski, Carolina Moore and Jenn Crookston for your help in writing this book. I seriously could not have done it without you!

To my family, thank you for putting up with my crafting madness and the extreme book deadlines. I love you all, and your support means the world to me.

Finally, to my followers, you are what makes a book like this possible. Your love and support on my videos, blog posts and social media are why I do this every day, and I can't thank you enough. I get to craft for a living and inspire you to create. It is the best job in the world!

ABOUT THE AUTHOR

Angie Holden has been blogging about all things Cricut for over a decade. She is the creative mind behind The Country Chic Cottage and creates inspirational projects daily. Angie lives on a farm in rural Tennessee with her husband, three children and three grandchildren. If she is not crafting, you can probably find her working on a ridiculously hard puzzle, playing '80s video games or hanging out with her family.

This book grew over the past decade from a love of creativity and all things Cricut. Angie has spent many hours crafting with her Cricut machines and perfecting techniques on a variety of projects. Now you can use her knowledge to get started creating with your machine!

Follow Angie on YouTube or on social media @countrychiccottage for more inspiration and creativity with your machine. Feel free to email angie@thecountrychiccottage.net with any questions about this book or the files that are used for the projects. Want to show off your creations? Be sure to use #cricuthandbook and tag Angie when posting on social!

INDEX